A WORLD REMEMBERED

Justine Chase

PAINTINGS BY ELSIE ROWLAND CHASE

DRAWINGS BY JOHN HAWKWOOD

Margery U. Ekwurtzel

Point O' Woods

1981

YANKEE BOOKS

A Division of Yankee Publishing Incorporated

Dublin, New Hampshire

First published in the United States in 1980 as
Document of a Child
by William L. Bauhan, Publisher
Dublin, New Hampshire

© 1988 Savitri Books Ltd (this edition and this design)
© 1988 Justine Chase (text)
© 1988 John Hawkwood (pencil drawings)

Library of Congress Catalog Card Number: 87–050775
ISBN: 0–89909–153–9
D. L. B-45.004-87
SIRVEN GRAFIC Gran Via 754 - Barcelona

Across the Chatham fields

This book was produced and designed by
Savitri Books Ltd
71, Great Russell Street
London WC1B 3BN
for
Yankee Publishing Incorporated
Dublin, New Hampshire

Art direction and book design: Mrinalini Srivastava

Printed in Spain

To Anne with love

PREFACE

I don't know if they neglect it, or their childhood is dim, or they feel it is hardly worth mentioning, but people seldom talk about when they were little. Yet if someone happens to, they usually listen with particular attention—not just for who is talking, but for what is said. And this quick interest in even quite a trivial disclosure seems to be so spontaneous and real it shows, I think, that people want to be reminded what it was like to be a child, to feel alive to the experience of being one. It is this experience—the things that being a child meant—which I have tried to capture by describing accurately, and without prejudice of age, what stays most vividly in mind, trusting its original significance.

The several sections have been written off and on over many years. I wrote the first one toward the end of the Second World War, after revisiting with Teresa, the sister closest to me, a house we loved—the house that had until quite recently been our parents' winter quarters, ours to come to as we wished, and ours, long since, to be children growing up in.

Those early years were spent for the most part in New England, during the first quarter of this century.

Most proper names are changed, except where the story's sense or the public knowledge of a person requires real ones.

It is a great joy to me that this illustrated edition of the book should include many of my mother's fine paintings.

Justine Chase, 1987

Opposite: portraits of Terry and me.

ACKNOWLEDGEMENTS

Elsie Rowland Chase's paintings on pp. 4, 29, 72, 129 and 137 appear by kind permission of Mr. David Taylor and of his wife, the late Mrs. Jessica Taylor. The author and Savitri Books extend their heartfelt thanks to Mr. Taylor for his cooperation and help. The picture on p. 44 is reproduced by permission of Dr. John Haight. All other works by E. Rowland Chase that appear in this book are the property of the author.

T AND NEVER TO RETURN

T he room was small. It had no rugs, no curtains. It looked like all rooms in empty houses everywhere, the kind of room one rents in made-over flats because it has a fireplace and might be livable if it were fixed up. It had the same empty feeling, although strictly speaking it was not empty. The whole half on the window side was jammed with tables, and they had black dusty sewing machines on them. But the front half was clear, and the doors were open; the hearth was bare, and the inside of the fireplace black and cold behind it.

The sewing machines belonged to the Red Cross. World War II was going on, and the whole of the house was being used then as Red Cross headquarters. It was big and airy and well suited to the purpose, and we were glad to have it used so well. It was a good way for a house to end.

But it was strange to come back to, not having seen the change; and hard to believe, particularly this special room. It was mercilessly changed; it even seemed a different shape, and it had shrunk terribly.

The rest of the house had kept its size at least. From outside it had looked the same as ever, big and well proportioned, with clean plain lines, three-storied and painted light gray. It had been good to see it there on the steep bank above the street, before turning up the driveway to the most used rear entrance; and good, on going in, to discover most of it, even in bare official dress, much like itself; our house in uniform, but still our house. The library downstairs was as peaceful as ever, and it had not lost its spacious brown dignity. The long tables with the women working did not seem out of place, and when someone looked up and said, "Can I help you?" I was able to answer, "No, thanks. We're looking around," in an easy enough voice. We—my sister Teresa and I—had stopped a moment by the window seat. I would have liked to stay there. I wanted to sit and watch Linden Street again the way I did when I was little. It looked the same, and sounded as quiet. As ours had been a winter house, the window was kept closed, so the street always seemed silent. The silence made things unreal but, in a way, clearer.

Things were always happening beyond that window-pane. The horses often fell on the icy hill. It was agony watching one slip; and try again; and slip again; until at last it went down, still struggling. One day a postman went by, weaving and bumping against the iron fence. It was the first time I ever saw a person drunk. Miss North, our governess, was watching too. She said it was sad to see a man in uniform in such a state. I thought about it a lot. Across the street lived a woman who was an invalid and who, Teresa told me, would die at once if she came outside. We both believed it, and I shall never forget the terrible moment when we saw her in her garden—sauntering!

That window seat was a perfect place to watch for the car. I would wait for it there to come back from the station, with Mother home from New York or my brothers from school. It disappeared round the corner of the house after that, then went by the French windows across the room, to the porte cochere beyond. There was time to run to the French windows and bang on them and wave, or, depending on who was coming home, to run very fast to the door.

And there, against the big brown cushions, I used to pore long hours over *Punch*. I knew the advertisements so well that, when I first went to London, with delight I found a carpet shop exactly where it should be, "under the shadow of Saint Paul's." I knew Johnny Walker whiskey, and a raincoat place, and I concluded rather sadly that most English people slept with their teeth beside the bed, the teeth obligingly "cleaning themselves" in a tumbler all night. But the English used Pear's soap, and so did we, and Eno's—in fact, they were much like us. This was reassuring, because I loved them so, and every secret hero I made up stories about was, as a matter of course, an Englishman.

I read every story, every joke, in every edition. I loved the drawings of the long-legged children my own age. They had straight hair, cut without a parting, and slim pretty mothers in jumpers and skirts who were usually "talking to Cook." And I remember laughing aloud to myself over: "Wanted: woman to sew buttons on the second floor."

Of course the whole house was queer, now that it was not lived in any more, but going through it again was not as bad as I had expected. It was only upstairs, as I stood in the room that had grown little, that I wanted to cry. It was the only room in the house that had changed completely. And it was one that should not have.

It had been a gracious, friendly room always, and now, so lately holy. For it was there that Mother had died not many months before, and it was there she lay the few last days before the funeral.

She looked as if she were resting then. There was a light counterpane across her feet of soft amber silk, and her dress was gray. A heavy silver brooch she had been fond of was at her neck, and on her breast the little purple ribbon, the gift of her beloved France. Mother did so many things so quietly, I have forgotten what the decoration was about. I think it was for helping a French village after the First World War. Anyhow, it was a nation's tribute to a friend whose compassion had been boundless, and to whom France had been singularly allied in spirit and thought.

~ 12 ~

We hung the portrait she had painted of her father over the bed. She had loved and admired deeply the clergyman and scholar whose beautiful collection of books was all of him I ever knew. And because Davidge, my elder brother, was in China, we put his photograph on the mantelpiece, so he could share our vigil too. Oliver, my second brother, had to telephone the long, careful cable that Father wrote: "Your dear mother died quietly this afternoon. . . ." He had a bad time getting through it.

The room was full of daffodils and azaleas and all sorts of Easter flowers. We kept the pompous fancy wreaths down-stairs. I was laughing about a specially lavish one, describing it merrily as we arranged the room, when two men from the farm were shown in to pay their respects. They were grave and dignified of course, and they must have been shocked. I could not explain and felt badly.

Yet grief is free to laugh, I think, where there is no resentment, and one could not resent the fact that Mother had died. She would not have. In fact, she was almost as interested in dying as she had been in living. Everything was interesting to her always. Inside the cover of her jewel case we found a paper with two poems copied out. One, from the Sanskrit, she had had in her dressing-table mirror long ago when I was little. It started:

> Look to this day
> For it is life, the very life of life.
> In its brief course lie all the verities and
> Realities of your existence . . .

The other, which she must have known we would find at her death, began: "Grieve not for me who am about to start/a new adventure. . . ."

Those few days after she died her presence, always great, was overwhelming. It seemed, my brother-in-law said, as though the room were bulging, as though her spirit were too great for it to hold. We were standing in the driveway

~ 13 ~

looking up at the house, almost expecting the walls to bend.

I felt this power of personality even more acutely a little later. Father wanted one of us with her always until the funeral, so we divided each night, and from dark to early dawn once, I was aware, somehow, of the very essence of being. I have little mystic trust or experience; I have no notions how this essence came to me—out of heaven if you like, or her discarded mute body, or an infinite release of my own mind—but the absolute that *is* a person, that had comprised this beloved woman who lay dead, was purely there.

The house in town.

That night was wonderful beyond any earthly thing. And it was a sort of benediction. The awful hurt, and the tears that would not stop now that no one was there I must be brave for, were curiously separate, as if they belonged to someone else. Outside the spring rain fell, and the crocuses were growing under the window and around the trees where Mother had planted them the year before. When daylight came I could see them, faint and light against the brown winter grass.

John Hardwood, 1987

This had been a sickroom for six weeks before she died. The oxygen tank stood in the far left corner. All the time, night and day, it played a melody of dripping ice; brittle and light and always exactly the same. The tent was ominous and scared us when Teresa and I first saw it, as we came in to see Mother after our long journey home. She said a sort of goodbye to us that night, and we tried to tell her that that was foolish. At least I did. I think Terry was braver and more honest, as Mother deserved.

Mother knew she was dying even if the doctors did not. She never tried to pretend. She would soon be wearing a golden robe, she would say with a delighted chuckle. Her voice was so weak we could scarcely hear her.

For a while she was not fully conscious, and would only talk in French. It was probably to keep the nurses out of what she was thinking. She hated having them about and loved to perplex them. They thought she was completely out of her head.

Mother had moved to this room when she knew how sick she was. She had herself carried down the passage in a straight-back chair. The change was partly for convenience—the room was well equipped, with a dressing room and bathroom through a door close to the bed and, across from there, the "Blue Room" where a nurse could sleep—but I think she chose it more to be away from Father then. Way at the other end of the house, she would spare him all she could.

One day I was sitting opposite the bed when she woke up. I said, "Hello!" and she said, "Hello!" and we smiled at each other. That was all. She was very tired. I went downstairs. It was Sunday afternoon, rather late apparently, since my eldest sister, Bobbie, and her husband and their children, who used to come to Sunday dinner, had all gone home. My sister Alice, and Oliver and Anne, his wife, were in the library. I joined them. Mother died ten minutes later.

~ 16 ~

She was probably unconscious when we got to her. The nurse called us and met us in the passage.

"She's going!" she said.

"Is there anything to do?"

"No, just be with her."

I held her hand and hoped she might think it was Father holding it. Perhaps she did.

Father was in the country paying a visit somewhere with Terry, who was called to the telephone while they were there. She had to tell him the dread news on the way back to town. Poor, darling Terry.

Here, where the oxygen tank stood, the doll's house used to be long ago. The room had been a nursery when Terry and I were little. Terry, who was nearly three years more

Above: still life.

grown up than I, slept in the "Blue Room" next to it.

What I remember most in the nursery, besides the doll's house, was a square brown bureau to the right of my bed. It was the last thing I could see at night. I would watch it turn gray, and then it was black, and then only its corner showed against the window, and then it disappeared.

We were allowed to talk a little after we went to bed. Terry would call from the next room, "Jan, have you got your pistol?" and I would say, "Yes, under my pillow. Have you got yours?" and she would say, "Yes, under my pillow, too." That would scare the burglars.

They haunted us sometimes, though. I remember trying to wake up from a nasty dream: I was down in the day nursery, and a burglar had climbed through one of the windows and, crouching behind me, was prying me from under the big easy chair with a blunt pitchfork. I had another nightmare at that time, one that kept coming back. Something horrible was chasing me up long flights of steps, and Terry and Miss North were at the top, leaning down to help me. But try as I would I could not reach their hands.

It was probably "Black Mary" who was after me. I think she was responsible for many nightmares. She was really my brother Davidge with boxing gloves on, huge awful black ones. Oliver would cry, "Black Mary! *Run!*" and Terry and I would grab his coat and we would tear through the house with Dav behind us, those black swollen mittens missing us by hair-raising inches.

But sometimes, before I went to sleep, a sort of waking nightmare overwhelmed me. This had nothing to do with Black Mary, and it was very much worse. I was, in fact, attacked, with relentless insistence, by the cosmic discomfort of logical thought; and if the logic seems foolish today, it was stunning then.

Adults, having traveled far from their source, have got thoroughly accustomed to their surroundings, so it is hard for me now to tell or understand wholly what I suffered. But it went, in present words, somewhat like this: "I am here, a conscious thing. My consciousness is I. I am inside my skull. I cannot get out. And so I can't be anybody else; can't be aware *in* anybody else to prove that anybody else is conscious too. Therefore, it follows, inescapably, that my own mind is all I *know* exists."

At this point my heart would stop. The possible conclusion was too horrible. I would try to put it out of my head, try not to think. It was no use.

"Maybe nothing else does exist! Maybe nothing anywhere is real but me. Maybe Terry and Mother and Father and everyone are make-believe. Maybe I pretend the world!"

I would sit up straight, staring at the dark; at the fireplace I could not see; at the doll's house and the bureau near the windows; all supposed to be there, all equally invisible. Who could help me? Whoever I questioned might not even be. A made-up person, a made-up answer; no help there. There was only myself to ask, "Am I all there is?" and only myself to answer. But these attacks did not come very often, thank God, nor the sleeping nightmares either, and the dark was friendly as a whole in that room; and I liked it.

When we had had a fire there were pleasant small noises of ashes settling in the grate, and often I went to sleep with the sound of the piano coming from far away downstairs. Mother used to play just before dinner. She played things like "The Mill," nothing very much, but I loved to listen.

And it was a nice room to wake up in: serene and soft gray in the early dawn. Out of the window I could see my aunt's snowy garden and look across the trees to the station tower and the clock. I could hear the trains come in when the wind was right, and I could see the smoke go up high, and at seven all the far factory whistles started at once. Here, no matter what the dark could threaten, were custom

and security hard to deny. I was not haunted by any doubts of daytime.

Teddy had to do with early morning then. I used to lie and watch him on the bureau. He was tiny and white and sat up very straight. He was my first visible friend in the early light. But perhaps it is my conscience that sees him there so clearly outlined alone against the sky. It was after our close friendship was done that he stayed there so much.

At first we went together everywhere. He used to ride in my mackinaw pocket on long, cold afternoons up and down the garden path. He ate with me, and slept with me, and he fitted nicely in my hand. I loved him with the tenderness and excitement and joy of discovery a child has in a new center of devotion. Then Miss North took him away. It was a punishment, I have forgotten why. But when she gave him back a week later, something dreadful had happened. I did not feel the same way any more. I liked him; I was glad to have him back; but for no understandable reason, the happiness had left. Our relationship had been cut off when it was full of promise. Now the time was gone. I could not get it back to that high, lovely level again. I felt sick with disappointment, and miserably deficient.

The Connecticut winters were long and cold. Some days we did not go outside. The icy air came to us instead right in the nursery. The nursery doors would be closed, the windows opened wide, and dressed in warm coats, we would play. The icicles dripped on the windowsills. The cold made the room a different place. The change was fun.

We almost always played with the doll's house then. It was a wonderful building. Our nurse Elleda—pronounced Elleeda and sometimes called "Lee" for short—had a brother, Carl, who made it for us. It opened on two sides so we could both play at once without a fight.

The doll's house family were named Baum in honor of the author of the Oz books. They had a blond tin limousine they rode in, all over the brown rug, very fast, and a lean greyhound who stood near the front porch.

The house had real electric lights, unheard of in those days, put in by an electric company that borrowed it once for a parade. The little house rode up Linden Street all lit up

Opposite: Terry playing patience.   ~ 21 ~

on a float while we watched enchanted. And once a carpet place sent Mother sample rugs, tiny Oriental ones just doll's house size. She let us have them.

Among the various events in the lives of the Baums, one stands out always in my mind. After a long and awful illness, a lady of the family died, and she was right in the middle of having a grand funeral when we got her mixed, and buried someone else. That day when we went down to lunch there was a paper propped on the table with something written on it in Bobbie's hand:

> Did you ever hear the story
> Of the lady who though dead
> Climbed up beside the driver
> As he gently shook his head,
> And glancing down beside her
> With a solemn wink she said,
> "Sh! The live one's in the dead box
> And they're burying her instead!"

The doll's house was big; there would be no place for it in the average room. It fills a great part of a large attic now. Yet the nursery contained it easily. Nothing was ever crowded there.

Sitting with two of "my children" in the nursery in town.

John Hawkwood

This had always been a generous room. There had been plenty of space for its full life, this small-looking Red Cross storeroom that I had come back to; this extra room, handy for sewing machines.

Terry and I stood near the threshold staring. She had seen the room already; she knew it was betrayed. When I muttered, "Oh, dear!" and turned away, blinking, she said, "Jan, don't. Someone might come in." Her voice was stern and did me good.

Of course, whoever did come in might generously impute a more suitable disaster to the poor lady than just the loss of an empty room. And no one coming into a Red Cross sewing room on a proper errand at high noon could suspect that the woman who turned tearfully away was wishing he would stumble.

~ 24 ~

Davidge used to trip across that doorway on a make-believe string. It was at night; we were in bed by then, and the room was dark. At the threshold he would pause and plunge. "Who put that *string* across the door?" he would say. It was an endless perfect joke.

Back from school between terms, he and Oliver decided "the babies" ought to use their heads, and they came upstairs every evening to see that we did. We had to learn things by heart to recite on command, later, in chorus, at table. There was a paean about an engine Ol had bought for his boat and had sweated over and cursed at all the past summer: "A two-cycle, reversible gasoline motor, easy to operate," it claimed, "clean to handle." This was flagrantly untrue, as was the further notion "carries like a satchel." It carried, when at all, like a wardrobe trunk. Yet we quoted the long sanguine piece faithfully, letter and spirit perfect.

Usually, however, it was poetry we learned, with suitable gestures added, as: "Fair is foul and foul is fair:/Hover through the fog and [here we held our noses] *filthy* air."

These assignments were part of the lovely game of obeying and humoring our brothers, and once the lights were out we waited in delight for the sound of their coming. Silhouettes would appear at last in the doorway against the glow of the passage, and then, always, Davidge would stop and stumble. So, on this day long after, a make-believe string was as present to my mind as the doorway before me. It was the same with everything; what had happened in this room was going on everywhere around me.

Over there two little girls sat face to face in silence. Miss North was a little way off, sitting equally still. The sitting and the stillness were the way we were punished when our spirits went embarrassingly high. It was discouraging how it always worked. No matter how hard we tried not to be subdued, we were. "Ida is a baby! She has on a long white dress! She's got a long white dress, so she's a baby!" We had

Opposite: the first portrait in my nurse's arms.   ~ 25 ~

been shouting to Ida the waitress down the backstairs.

And there in front of the empty hearth we pranced before the blaze with nothing on, our undershirts warming on the firescreen, and Elleda repeating with unremitting hope: "Who's going to get dressed first? Who's going to win?"

And here to the right of the dressing-room door my dear baby Ethel broke her head the morning after Christmas on the bars of my crib. She was china and only a day old.

When the crib was outgrown, my bed was placed about where I now stood. This was the side I got in, where I used to say my prayers; where often when I should have been in bed, I was found in rapt devotion, after a mad dash from Terry's room at the sound of someone coming. A small child praying, though flushed and strangely breathless, could not decently be scolded.

There was a straight cane-seated chair this side of the bed where I remember pondering about Martha and Mary. It was Sunday evening after Mother had been reading to us. I was taking off my shoes.

The trouble about Martha and Mary was that I was Martha. Of course, Terry was obviously Mary, whether I was there or not. I was solemnly aware that Terry was blessed; she was special and fine. Fine outside as well as in; Ivory soap was too strong for her, Elleda said, and she was born on Sunday. It all had to do with her soul somehow, along with her goodness.

My soul was full of petty duties. If Jesus came to call, I would try to pick things up, while Terry would have the heart and sense to listen. Terry was Mary; I was Martha. I did not want to be Martha. I hated it. But I knew I was.

For a while there was a long looking glass by the door to Terry's room. I remember Alice mirrored there in her wedding dress.

Alice had just got back from the war when she married.

She had been a Red Cross nurse in Paris, a volunteer out of college, terribly young. It was to Paris badly wounded men in World War I were mostly sent, rushed by the thousands from the trenches. Lives depended on good nursing, and Alice, we were told, was so efficient that she had been recommended for a medal. I was proud of her, of course, but rather worried privately that she might come back in heavy stockings and sensible shoes. Miss North was to blame. I think she resented Alice's prettiness and chic and many beaux. She thought her unstable. It must have been provoking to have her proven hardy. Alice would come back changed, she said. And as of course Miss North meant she would be more like Miss North, I was uneasy.

But she had not changed a bit. In fact, she smoked. Furthermore, she was engaged to marry a hero, an ace in the Lafayette Escadrille. Better still, the hero's closest friend, another hero, had fallen in love with Alice too. And they asked him to be best man at the wedding. Would he accept? The air was tense. He did.

So we watched lovely Alice, Terry and I, while Elleda fixed her veil. We were waiting for the car to take us to All Saints', two gangling little bridesmaids in huge pink hats.

Somehow the price tag got left on my hat and it dangled down my back all afternoon. I must have been altogether an odd sight that day. My face was very red. We had to stand in the receiving line for a long time, suffering a vast amount of kisses. I felt awfully queer, worse all the time, but not till the last unwitting guest had left did the family look at me more closely. I was redder than ever; I had a bad sore throat; I had a high fever—I had the measles.

Being sick in the nursery was a cheerful event, unless, of course, one felt particularly ill. Usually it was just a bad cold, with steam kettles and sniffles. The sun poured in across the snowy winter, and the fire was burning, and people came to say hello or to read out loud. When Terry and I were ill at the same time, we had a basket that went back and forth on a string from her room to mine carrying treasures.

One day I was given ether in that room; I had to have an operation. Afterwards I traveled disembodied up the bed, the wrong way round, feet toward the pillow. It was an easy, slow sail. I recall it with pleasure frequently. When I opened my eyes I was back in place again. Mother was beside me holding my hand, where I had left her before the anesthetic. She and the doctor were looking at me, smiling. I remember trying to tell them what had happened, but my tongue was dry, and I gave up. I remember the helpless and familiar feeling of communication thwarted.

There were countless barriers, in those days, to making oneself understood to grown-ups; it was very discouraging. We forgave legitimate obstructions. It was hard to talk to Father and Mother sometimes, because of being shy, but the fault was ours, we saw it and accepted it. Governesses and nurses often ruined conversation on the finish-your-milk-first-please principle; this was maddening, but one knew the reason for it. Besides, a statement once achieved in front of parents or nurses was heeded and given credence.

This was not so, however, with other grown-ups. They were always unpredictable. Their attention and their beliefs were equally unstable, which made talking to them harassing, sometimes hopeless. There was their puzzling carelessness; they would ask things and then forget to listen. One would get all ready to answer, and find it was too late.

But their most annoying habit, in the frustration it begot, was a result of willful innocence. They had ideas, because they wanted to have, of what a child was thinking. Nothing one could say would change their minds. One was curiously helpless: "She is wondering . . ." or "She wants . . ." or

~ 28 ~

"She is feeling . . .," and they would add some foolish thing
not true at all.

Once they told me that as soon as I was seven all my hair
was going to fall out. I laughed as I was meant to, yet it was
promptly stated: "She believes it!" Right up to my birthday
they hounded me with: "The poor child is worrying about
her hair." Denial only bored them. There were other fibs
like that, which they would go back to over and over with
immense enjoyment. But the joy, it seemed to me, was at

Above: portrait of my father.

their own expense; they made themselves not only trying but ridiculous.

Besides the ways one was to think, they had ways one was to look. They were so eager it was tempting to indulge them. I remember being asked on a wonderful morning if I would like to go to Coney Island, too? It was after several hints, and I had been hoping. We were at table, and everyone beamed and watched me. They nudged each other and leaned forward to see my pleasure. The pleasure was there, and it was strong, but it did not show the way they wanted. So, I made my eyes shine—I remember the process clearly—like a well-trained actor, deliberately. "Look at her," they cried in satisfaction. "Just look at her eyes *shine*!"

So one learned to humor adults and to treat them deviously the way they seemed to like.

They were sometimes uncivil. "Come, little girl," a visitor would say, "come and sit on my lap." And then: "Good heavens! Please get off, dear! The *white* comes off your shoes!" It was highly insulting. I can see Teresa tumbling off a dark blue knee of someone sitting near the nursery window, someone with blue serge trousers and a hand brushing madly.

In our general contempt for grown-up manners, Father and Mother were hardly included. They did not act like fools.

Our knowledge of Father was mostly in the library, or out riding in the country, and rather remote. But though Mother was not actually with us much, our connection was close. Her influence colored those nursery days with lovely warmth and richness. And to be with her was impressive, particularly so, because our nurses always did the ordinary things and she always did the special ones. That meant that she was there when we wanted her most. I do not know how she managed it, considering all she was besides our mother, but she never, ever failed any one of six children.

~ 30 ~

She lived her private life, her public life, her social life, her artist's life, all without skimping.

So whenever we saw her, it counted; whether she was ministering to a bloody knee, or teaching us to pray, or reading aloud in her quiet pretty voice—or whether we came formally to dine, by written invitation!

"To meet Miss Hathaway," the little card said. I have it pasted in my scrapbook. Miss Hathaway was Trudy, a playmate. It was very exciting. We dressed up like grown-up ladies, came to the front door, were shown into the reception room, and properly announced. I sat up straight on a delicate gold chair, and Mother asked me gravely, "What do you think of the purple wigs they are wearing now in Paris?"

But most of our dressing up was for plays, and these were presented in the nursery. I remember striding to and fro past the fireplace, or trying to, in Father's rubber boots. I was a somewhat nervous Bluebeard at that moment because "sister Anne" was late, and silences were bad. They could be filled too easily with: "Children, isn't that a guest-room bedspread?"

Perhaps because the maids were our best audience I see myself as if at the same time reciting carefully –for the glory of Elleda, and, manifestly, me—the Lord's Prayer in Swedish to Sofia, the cook. Pictures come to mind with no regard to proper sequence when one starts remembering.

The room itself changed character many times. After it was not a nursery any more it belonged for a while to Granny. She used it as a sitting room where she had her desk and books. We still spent happy times in it. She read Dickens to us there.

Later it was a room that was all dressed up. I was moved back to it once. It had twin beds, and taffeta quilts, and a real chaise longue. It had a bed table and a lamp. I read *Uncle Tom's Cabin* late every night, and wept in luxury.

~ 31 ~

At first, long ago, before the wing was added, it was Mother's and Father's room. Those of us with winter birthdays must have been born there.

A good place to be born in, and to grow in, and to die; dear, ample, friendly room. It probably was better after all, I felt, that it should end entirely; and good—I *tried* to feel—that this small room which had taken its place belonged at least to something purposeful and generous.

We stood still in the sunlight that came through the bare windows, Terry and I together. Then she said, "We'd better go."

With my dog Zoë and little Kim.

A FOND ACQUAINTANCE

"H ow many people do you know?" Teresa would ask, and I would start counting. I always began with Miss Kingston, whom I scarcely knew at all. She was one of Mother's friends and lived in a house we walked by on our way downtown. Perhaps she represented the outside world, or perhaps she came to mind because the first time Terry asked me we were watching Mother on her way to pay a call. We were looking out of the window as she walked across the drive, to "see Miss Kingston," Elleda said. This was a part of Mother's life I had not considered. I tried to picture it exactly.

I never finished all the people I knew, but I always started carefully with the various acquaintance of the household staff, after Miss Kingston. Next came the men who worked on the farm, Chatham, where we lived in summer, and I do not think I ever went any further.

So whenever I recall the background of those days, and the people who filled it, Teresa's question comes to mind again, and the maids and men at home. As houses and estates during and after World War I were still securely and abundantly attended, I was surrounded by many persons. I do not remember them as well-rounded characters; we did not see people that way, but as pieces of separate experience encountered day by day. As incidents, as feelings, as discoveries, as friends, they filled my early world with warmth and interest.

Sofia, the cook, was plump and Swedish. She had trouble sometimes with butcher knives. "Sofia's cut her finger again!" would bring us rushing to watch it bleed. She was jolly and laughed a lot; she was a dear friend of Elleda's, and she loved to sing. She sang a strong soprano that carried the hymns on Sunday mornings. We had church at home in the summer. Father read the morning service; Mother played the hymns; the Kirks, close neighbors, climbed the hill to join us. At ten o'clock Dav and Ol, Terry and I, the two Kirk girls, and any other children present took different-sized bells from a shelf in the living room (though the "Big Room" was what we called it) and paraded through the whole house, ringing.

The family, the maids, the Kirks, and weekend visitors made a fair congregation. The dogs were there too; Beda, the Russian wolfhound, away on the sofa, removed but listening, and Kim, the Boston bulldog, in the thick of things by the piano. I was usually next to Miss North, of course. I could sing tolerably, and she tried to persuade me to hold my head up and sing right out. This was exactly what I longed to do, but since she asked me to, I would not. Besides, the boys would have complained. They scorned little singing sisters. Sofia had no such problems. She sang out generously.

It is good to recall her. She always had to do with pleasant things. If I stood beside her while she drank a cup of coffee she would dip a lump of sugar in the cup, and as soon as it was deep beige halfway up she would give it to me. It was lukewarm on my tongue and delicious. I would let it crumble slowly.

And Sundays in the country, when she had finished the ice cream, she let Terry and me lick the freezer clean. We sat outside on a brick floor where it could drip without a fuss—a place used mainly for deliveries, near the kitchen. It was a lovely interval between suffering a walk and being put in clean frocks for Sunday dinner.

I remember a delightful snapshot of Sofia. Father took it I think. She is standing beside the kitchen table, smiling

~ 34 ~

fondly at a roast suckling pig with an apple in its mouth. The crisp little pig is smiling too.

When Sofia married she left us. I went to her wedding with my parents and Teresa. It was in a church that to me did not look like a church; it was golden oak inside. Elleda was maid of honor. She stood directly in front of us, and beyond the top of my prayer book I could see her arm shaking all through the service. At the end the minister asked Father and Mother to address the congregation. Mother turned to Father, and Father rose. He must have said what I thought he should; I do not remember feeling at all uneasy.

We had a young French nurse, Simone, who got married too around that time. Her wedding was at All Saints', our church, so it seemed more real. She was a delicate lovely bride, and she walked up the aisle in the special way she had practiced in the nursery. A hesitating step was proper, she had said, and every step, she paused, and then swung her ankle in, before going on.

She married one of the campers who came to the lake in the summer, a good man, I think, but her happiness ended. She took to running away and riding downtown on a truck, her hair loose and flying. They brought her back to him and she quieted a little, but not for long. Finally I suppose, she was officially locked up. She had been a gay person. It was sad and strange.

Ida, the waitress, came from Norway. She skated beautifully. In town, the boys used to flood the lawn, and it made a decent rink. There Ida, previously restricted in white cotton, turned into a swift, curving creature. She was, for a metamorphic moment, enchanting. Otherwise she was grim, especially to children. This gave her a vital place in Terry's life and mine. Ida was our focus of aggression. Ida was our foe. She goaded us and we goaded her, and we accepted punishments for rudeness, but never gave up.

~ 35 ~

I cannot remember much about our fights with her, more about the feelings that went with them: the compulsion to bully and be scared, to torment and retreat. We felt obliged to behave like brats; being in Ida's way was irresistible, hiding from her or fooling her an unending pleasure.

At our Chatham seat in summer we had a favorite hiding place. There was a deep top shelf in the pantry store closet with room for us behind the rows of olives. Getting up on it took careful climbing and tedious moving of jars, which we replaced one by one to screen us. The closet light had a long cord and a wire guard around the bulb. We pulled it after us; it made things bright and warm. We used to tap the back wall there in search of a secret room the boys said was somewhere in the house. Hollow sounds and uncharted spaces were beyond, but no magic door sprang open. Even so, this was a good place to be. We were in a world of subtle and delicious smells; smells of chocolate and spice, of nuts and preserves, and the brown clean wood of the shelf itself. We kept still, of course, speaking in whispers. No one whose footsteps went by busily below could desecrate our dwelling. No one in all the world, particularly Ida, could suspect that two small contented children lived way back up in that lovely place.

Nor did Ida know about our oven. She never thought to look inside. The little oven, supplied for keeping plates warm, was in the middle of the pantry radiator. It was the kind of thing nobody used, and the neat iron doors opened quietly, and Terry and I found it highly satisfactory for bread crusts. At Chatham we ate our supper in the pantry every night, so we got it stacked pretty high.

Nor did Ida know why the apples she chose from the cellar storeroom in town and placed carefully on the little dumb-waiter that went to the pantry turned rotten. When she pulled them up later they had turned bright brown. There were always brown ones somewhere in the barrel.

~ 36 ~

We took the squashiest and made a quick exchange. It troubled and perplexed her.

Many things that Ida did discover were hard for her to bear. One time she was wrong, a memorable occasion of justice and high triumph for Teresa. Ida found some curious and no doubt familiar marks around the icing of a cake she was to serve. She assumed we were to blame, of course, although for once we had not touched it. Terry told her we had not, but Ida did not believe her. Moreover, the apparent lie vexed her so highly that she stamped off to Mother, cake in hand. Her disbelief was natural, considering our past and the present indubitably thumby cake, but going to our mother about this sort of thing was overwhelming. Little Terry went too, crying and helpless. Ida showed the awful marks that Terry dared deny, and waited securely. "But Ida," Mother said, "Teresa says she did not do it." That was all.

Ida believed that Judgment Day was coming soon, on a specified date. When it got to be a few weeks away I too became uneasy. I knew I would not pass the Judgment well for one thing, and in any case, being on my own, without a family or even a world, would be utterly dreadful. I was pretty sure it would not happen, and it was comforting that no one else seemed concerned, outside the small mysterious sect that Ida followed. Yet true prophets had been ignored in every age. The day came . . . and went. And it was pleasant to go on, in the same place and the same world, even with Ida.

As we grew older, and probably less in the way, our feud with her tottered a little, so that when she came back from a visit to Norway with two tiny pitchers for our dolls, all we could do was surrender, abashed by the irregular behavior of the enemy.

For a while there was Hedvig, a parlor maid. Hedvig's significance in our lives was contradiction. She was important because she was not. There was so little to notice about her that she was remarkable. She had brownish hair, and a dim square for a face. Her expression never changed, and she rarely spoke. Dav and Ol promoted her vacancy enthusiastically: "What reminds you," they would suddenly ask, "of the blank side of a hill? *Perfectly* blank. *Nothing* on it?" The answer was always, "Hedvig's face!"

Another shadowy but memorable person was Sarah, the laundress. She was shadowy because she looked so very old and I was very young when she was with us; and she was memorable because I looked at her once so intently. She was standing in the sewing-room doorway in the dim light of the landing in town, and I wanted to see her accurately for two important reasons. She had had a dreadful operation—they had taken off one of her breasts—and she came from the Middle Ages; she had never learned to read. Sarah closed the door and went down the kitchen stairs, and I do not remember her again.

Delia, the Irish chambermaid, although a merry friend, was Terry's and my continual concern. For one thing, we had a lot of trouble trying to teach her French. We gave her columns of complicated words to learn by heart and a great many hopeful lessons, but though her patience and good humor were equal to the test, she was a disappointing student. She never got anywhere at all with her homework, and all she learned to say was "*Cela m'est égal,*" or, in her version, "Slam et gel!"

We led her a shocked life. I see her now, hands high in dismay, as we jumped on the beds with nothing on. Nakedness was sacrilege to Delia, a grave sin even when alone, for one never was actually alone on account of guardian angels. One's own private angel was always on hand, and mighty proper too. We asked her if it wanted her to take a bath with clothes on and I cannot remember her reply, but I always pictured her bathing in a sort of canvas shift.

~ 38 ~

Every year we made her a special Valentine. Terry made one and I made one, both alike, and always the same. When all the other Valentines were finished, we would say, "Now we must make Delia's." We would take two round brass ashtrays from the library table and trace circles. We drew eyes and nose and mouth inside, and that was all. I do not know why they were so fitting—Delia had a long bumpy face—but something about them seemed to catch her jovial spirit.

The mild and cheerful occupation of counting people I knew may have ended before Beth came, although Teresa kept me at my work off and on for years, I think. She would look at me severely at odd times, when we had nothing much to do for several minutes, and say, "*How* many people do you know? You never finished! Start again."

"Miss Kingston and Sofia," I would answer hastily, and I was off, and she sat back to listen.

The maids in the Chatham garden.

Beth was a chambermaid, too, so she must have come after Delia left; besides, my brothers were grown up and in college when she was with us. Beth was gentle, shy, and beautiful, one of the loveliest people I have ever known. Her skin was ivory color, and she had soft brown hair and a quiet slow, sweet smile, a smile that still gives me a feeling of repose.

To us she was always the tender pretty Beth of *Little Women*, except that we also had her in love with Ol. But that was in retrospect, long after she left and married and had her first son. Someone told us she had named the baby Oliver, and Terry and I hoped that could only mean that she had once adored Ol himself secretly. He was so much a person she would have been likely to love that our drama seemed credible.

Rachel, a kitchen maid, I remember through the glass

pane of a door. The memory is unpleasant because she was laughing at me. I was in the butler's pantry at Chatham, calling Terry. We had decided that morning to improve the English language by reviving the second-person singular, so I was shouting, "Terry! Oh Teresa! Where art thou?" when I noticed Rachel's glee and stalked away.

Kitchen maids came and went frequently. Some of them were odd. One, called Esther, was interesting because Elleda said she found her hiding chop bones.

One day, again at Chatham, as I went through the hall a new parlor maid was answering the doorbell. I started to run upstairs as a precaution against callers, when I heard my mother's voice outside. She was asking clearly and brightly if she (Mother) was at home. I came down again, fascinated. The new maid paused a second, and then said, "I'll see . . . Won't you please come in?" and stepped aside politely. Mother said something else, and the girl went off looking pleased. I do not remember which maid this was, but I connect answering doorbells with Priscilla. Yet surely had she been Priscilla, I could not have forgotten it.

Priscilla fluttered. She was overpoweringly tentative. She stood like a bird about to take off, and walked on tiptoe, swaying forward. Her hands were suspended in front of her somehow, and she talked in a voice that went back up; it was whispery, and she simpered with it.

Priscilla came on Sundays at first to help serve; later she was a constant member of the household. She was a kind, good person, serious inside. And if one noticed it, she was handsome. Dressed for the street she looked very much a lady. Davidge used to mix her up with Mrs. Barnes, a family acquaintance and neighbor not unlike Priscilla in appearance. Her manner, to our taste, was so oversweet it was like Priscilla's simper. In hats, according to Davidge, the two women were identical. He was always meeting one of them on Linden Street. If he said, "Good morning, Mrs.

Opposite: one of the maids.   ~ 41 ~

Barnes," she would chirp, "Oh! Good morning, Mr. Davidge!" If he said, "Good morning, Priscilla," she would coo, "Why Davidge, *dear*! How *are* you?"

Priscilla was continual entertainment. We mimicked her unmercifully. We would hover through a room with idiotic smiles or stand, looking tentative. They were good imitations. We were like her.

Yet Mother painted her picture. And it is like her. She is in profile on her knees in church, holding a rosary in strong, interesting hands. She is looking down. Light pours across her face, modeling its fine and definite planes, and heightening a look of contemplation that is wholly compelling. It is a noble and thoughtful and terribly sad face, very beautiful.

Elleda was the hub of the backstairs world, and as she was our nurse off and on for many years, she was a vital part of Terry's life and mine. Yet I cannot isolate Elleda to see her clearly as she was when I was little. She belonged to the household before I did, and I always knew her. She came when she had just turned seventeen and never left us. After Father died more than sixty years later, and she herself was getting old and ought to have rested, we remodeled a farm cottage and retired her to live in it, but her retirement meant little; her concern was still to do what she decided needed doing for the family—any member of it in reach. She lived to be past eighty, a life tirelessly kind, beloved and indispensable.

It was mostly through her eyes that we followed the events of the busy kitchen wing. She made it seem a gay and hearty place. We envied its life sometimes. It was a place where jokes were always being played, things like pulling rugs from under people's feet. Sofia was usually responsible. She was a great one for every sort of practical joke, abetted by Elleda.

And when the maids had visitors they played delightful

games like "clap in and clap out"; Elleda taught it to us. It was partly a game and partly a jig and lots of fun. In the country, around a piano, they had lively times singing songs and eating Swedish cakes. If we stood in the back passage and listened down the stairs we heard their voices. Sometimes we caught snatches of stories they were telling that left us tantalized: "And dere I vas on my hands and knees laffin' fit to kill!" was food for happy contemplation. In the evening if I came to ask Elleda about something it was hard to find a lull in which to call her, the sitting-dining-room was so full of laughter and talk. I felt timid about coming straight down to the closed door, and waited in the middle of the stairs till someone finally heard my patient summons.

At Chatham when the girls went out they had breathtaking adventures at night with the Hathaway cows. The Hathaways lived a mile or so away if you took the shortcut across the fields, and their maids and ours saw each other often, a hair-raising feat. Every cow was in every field they had to cross, elephants in the dark with wet noses. It meant running for dear life away from them and headlong into them. To this day my heart beats fast at the thought of a Hathaway cow. It is no relation to a usual cow at all. It is a wild, nocturnal, stalking, awful thing.

If one of the maids had a birthday coming, a party would be planned weeks ahead. It was always to be a surprise and took a lot of cunning. The protagonist was overwhelmingly astonished when the exciting moment came: "You should have seen her face!" Elleda would tell us. We would wonder, considering Elleda, how anyone could have been deceived. Elleda, planning surprises, had a glad and foolish smile. We knew it so well we could spy it instantly when it had to do with us, so she would try to control it by looking what she considered woeful. She would look so astonishingly guilty instead that we suspected her, of course,

and we would chant, "Oh, there's something queer about Elleda!" We would watch her mouth till the corners of it twitched, and then shout, "There's the smile!"

Most of her surprises were delightful, but there was one I dreaded. On dinner-party nights she brought lovely treats upstairs, like banana ice cream, my favorite, or little square cakes, cold and delicious with silver dots on green icing. But sometimes she brought us one great oyster each. It was Terry who liked oysters. I wanted to be sick whenever I saw one, yet the notion having started that an oyster was a treat, I would chew the thing valiantly until it had no taste, and swallow it in dogged, tense installments.

The maids had many beaux. At Chatham they came courting in the dusk. On warm summer evenings if we crossed the back croquet course when it had got too dark for them all to play, we would hear quiet voices and gay little laughs from the kitchen porch. One or two of the girls would be sitting in the shadows with their suitors. And someone inside would be playing the piano, some pleasant sentimental song or the tune of an evening hymn, tried slowly with one finger.

Our infrequent butlers never seemed to be about, nor to figure in Elleda's gay reports. They most likely used their free time hiding desperately from Ida. Butlers never weathered her for long. She could not put up with them, and did not.

One called Lazare was pale and had dark hair, and he shaved in the Latin way—his jaw was blue. I used to study it; it divided his face when he carried in the tea tray.

An extraordinary man was with us for a while. He was Greek and played a fiddle. Dav and Ol could hear him playing early every morning as loud as he knew how. They claimed he always opened with "The Star-Spangled Banner," knowing they were still in bed, to make them stand up. I remember him as "Aeolian," which he probably

Opposite: Terry.   ~ 45 ~

was not, but whatever his name, it suggested pagan Greece.

He was actually a singularly missionary Christian. He sent notes to Mother about true faith. He wrote on his days off and mailed his letters from New York. Sometimes he sent postcards. He wrote about heaven, and Jesus, and Davidge. How Davidge made the grade we never knew, or in what capacity. For when Dav, thus sanctified, had spent a few days away, there were flowers heaped around his place at table, and a big white card in Aeolian's careful printing said: "WELCOME TO THE PRODIGAL SON."

Aeolian loved flowers. He arranged them with tenderness and skill. The table, even without Dav as inspiration, was always covered with them. There were exquisite blossoms laid in lines along the cloth, as well as intricate and lovely center bouquets. He used to gaze from his window at Mother's garden. It was right below his room, the high tower room, our favorite in the house. One dark night as he was deep in contemplation two phantoms appeared below. They were dressed in white and they danced silently on the lawn between the paths. He stared stupefied till they vanished from sight. Then he went to find a human being. He was shaking when he met Elleda in the hall, and described what he had seen. Elleda guessed what sort of ghosts had been at large, and told us the story sternly the next day.

Teresa and I used to sneak out of bed on lovely summer nights and tiptoe cautiously away in nightgowns and bare feet. We went along the dim passage and down the first stairs, with only rare passersby to fear, but when we reached the landing, we were truly in peril. Light came through the Big Room doorway, exactly opposite, and if Mother was at her desk, our legs were in full sight. It took skill and good judgment to go down the last steps, holding absolutely still if boards were creaky, and then to move swiftly at the proper moment, and surely, and without a

~ 46 ~

sound. The dining-room doorway was next to the stairs; two steps and we would reach it, our hearts pounding. When we had got across the room, opened the screen door, and were beyond it on the porch, we were safe enough in the blackness, and we scampered, elated.

We would have made accomplished thieves; no one ever caught us on our way. We traveled by sound and particularly touch. I can feel the journey still through the soles of my feet. There was carpet from upstairs to the dining room; it was soft and stiff and pliant all at the same time. Then came a rigid narrow rise of threshold, and then smooth floor; a bumpy fringe, and a silky rug, the fringe, and smooth floor again; then the threshold to outdoors, complicated and scary. It was wider than the other and it humped up a level,

With Elleda.

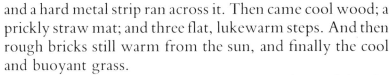

and a hard metal strip ran across it. Then came cool wood; a prickly straw mat; and three flat, lukewarm steps. And then rough bricks still warm from the sun, and finally the cool and buoyant grass.

The garden at night was mysteriously beautiful. The sward was velvet black, and so were the Japanese pine tree and the shrubs and the honeysuckle wall against the sky. The sky was black-gray, and the stars were yellow dots, and fireflies made quick bright sparks. The baby's breath beyond the path looked like white mist. The little fountain in the corner splashed faintly. There was no other sound. The smell of the roses was intoxicating. We would dance there, in whispers so no one could hear us, and creep back ecstatically to bed.

"Yanet, she comin'?" Ogard would ask Terry if I were not directly behind her. We used to copy the way he said it, the scoop and the lilt. Ogard was our Swedish chauffeur. He knew all about cars and was an excellent driver, but he never mastered English, especially road signs; he searched every road in Connecticut for years for a town called "CAU-TION." Like all self-respecting chauffeurs, he would rather get lost than ask for help, so we went, with much backing and turning, on unexpectedly long trips.

Ogard always reminded me of El Greco's Cardinal. There was a copy in the upstairs passage of the house in town. He wore the same kind of eyeglasses, and had the same nose, and his face was exactly the same color. When I try to recall it now, I see the print instead. I remember him best out of the corner of my eye, a dark figure in the dining room at breakfast time: he would come in and stand there, and I would grow fidgety waiting for Father to say, "Oh, Ogard! Good morning! I didn't see you there," and then, "Ethel, do you want the car today?"

I told a lie to Ogard once that I could not forget because it

~ 48 ~

proved I was not a man, but a mouse. I was sitting in the limousine one winter afternoon waiting with him in front of Father's office. We were talking about Christmas. I was planning what to buy, and counting up my money, and asking what various things were apt to cost. Teresa and I had recently achieved a ten-cents-a-month allowance. The first bright dimes had appeared one day, next to our plates at lunch. There were little brand-new notebooks too, for keeping accounts. Miss North had shown us about our credits and our debits, and we managed our incomes carefully. We felt well set up. So when Ogard asked how much I had for buying presents, I answered proudly, "I get ten cents every month." "Ho! Ho!" he laughed, "Ten *cents*? You mean of course ten dollars!" I encountered my reply before it came, and watched it, along with the back of Ogard's head and the rectangle beyond of winter sky. I remembered thinking what a weak, petty sort of lie it was, and wondering if I was really going to tell it, and answering with a laugh that made me squirm, "Yes, of course, I meant ten dollars!"

Through the summers our daily companion was Adolf, the groom. Castello came before Adolf, I think, and before Castello, Axel. But I was too young to know either of them well. I recall Castello only as a natty horseman who had hurdles put up on the north lot. My sister Bobbie, a keen rider, used to jump Bird there, a fine brown horse, Father's favorite.

Axel had a red moustache. On an afternoon when I was very little, I woke up on the middle of the stairs. I do not know why I was there—I had probably been waiting for Teresa. I only remember waking with someone bending over me, asking if I would like a ride. I was lifted up, still sleepy, and carried through the hall, out the door to the porte cochere. I was placed way on top of an auburn animal which carried me slowly round the drive. Axel walked close beside us. His head was no higher than my knee. I must have been impressed by my bird's-eye view, because all I remember of my first ride on a horse, beyond sleepiness and bright sun, is Axel's red moustache below me all the way.

It was Adolf who taught Terry and me how to ride, who accompanied us across the green hills, and talked life over with us on the way. He had been in the Swedish cavalry, where he rode at breakneck speed, jumping fences. They were wire fences, hard for a horse to see. They had to be made visible, he told us, so when you came to one, you ripped off your coat, leaped to the ground, and threw the coat across the wire. You mounted, retreated, turned, and took the fence, then galloped back and leaped to the ground again—snatched the coat, hurled it on, mounted on the run, dashed along to the next fence, and began all over. We listened eagerly, out of breath.

Adolf's favorite dish was corned beef and cabbage. I had never tasted either one. My ignorance pleased me, I re-member; it seemed to stress my higher rank. At that age we were snobs about the unfamiliar unless it came from a venerated source. Had Adolf been a prince or English, two equal conditions to my mind, I would have felt bound to know and like and eat what he did. But for everyday people, my criterion was smug: what I was not used to, I scorned.

Besides, Adolf was worse than everyday people. He smelt of sweat and boots. Social difference where Adolf was concerned was largely olfactory. Once I heard of a lady who ran off with a groom. This was interesting, for Adolf was good-looking. Terry and I talked it over thoughtfully. We decided, however, that no matter what was stated, it could not possibly be true—unless, of course, they lived in the open air.

~ 50 ~

We admired Adolf, though, and thought him every inch a man. So when our country went to war, and Adolf went home, we were miserably ashamed. The instant war was declared, it was said, he scurried back to Sweden.

The Italians on the farm were our friends too. They were gay, dark people who sang when they drove by and put roses behind their horses' ears. There were Big Jo and Angelo and Little Jo and Franky and Tony and two Mikes.

One still summer's day Terry and I were playing house, or maybe just spying, behind some bushes, when Big Jo came trudging by along the quiet road. And then, all at once, his wife was there, screaming. Italian words rushed out of her mouth, faster and louder, with incredible crescendo. Her hands tore the air. She was like an ancient fury, violent, primordial. I held my breath, frightened. At last she stopped. Then she turned, and strode to the field, and was gone as quickly as she came. Everything was still; the world was perfectly at ease; Big Jo was trudging up the quiet road.

The Italians gave us coins with square holes in the middle when Teresa and I played "pilgrims," a game that meant

Ogard with his pride and joy.

journeying abroad with bundles on canes. We would each shoulder a walking stick of Father's upside down, with a tam-o'-shanter hanging off the tip. The tams were our bundles and standard equipment for our victuals. As soon as we were hungry we settled in a tree, preferably at the top, and fared greedily on Maillards's chocolate and Educator crackers.

Our route always took us down the north road, till we found a proper tree to stop in, then on by the horses' drinking trough in the woods, and past the Italians'. Then we climbed the steep, curving wood road by the brook, and went to a great spreading maple with a bench around it. A spring rose next to it, and cold water trickled out of a rusty pipe. A china mug hung from a nail; we stopped to quench our thirst there. Then on we went up the hill into the sun, past the stable, past the dairy. Up the east drive, and over the lawn, and onto the verandah. And into the cool hall: home.

The Italians' house was thin and brown and built against a hill. Several families lived in it on different floors. In the dark of the wood, the foreign voices made it strange. If we were feeling timid we went by without stopping, but generally adventure mastered fear, and we knocked on the door and held out our hands, on the fruitful assumption that pilgrims should be beggars. Whoever opened the door, Mike or Joe or Angelo—our excitement made them all the same—met us with a merry laugh and spoke in quick Italian to the others inside. They would all come out then, and laugh too, and go in again, to fetch the curious, enchanting coins. There were brown coins and gray coins, little ones and big. We put them in our tams, delighted.

I remember the other men on the farm mainly because of fascinating troubles. We held Charlie, the painter, in close attention and respect because he would "die young," he declared. Painters, it seemed, always did; they filled their lungs with lead. And Rich, the jolly handyman, had one arm missing, and Dewey, the dairyman, had no right eye.

And then there was Mr. Martin's heart! It was in a dreadful state. Mr. Martin, the carpenter, was a man of privilege, but just why was a matter of rude conjecture:

> Oh it's, "Angelo get the garbage,"
> And it's, "Dewey clean the sink,"
> But it's, "Thank you, *Mister* Martin,
> For the very pretty pink!"

. . . Dav and Ol used to sing. Besides his title, and his heart, and his rare working hours (he was an intermittent carpenter at best), Mr. Martin lived in the most distinguished little house on the place. It was the house where LaFayette had spent the night and where his staff had drunk hard cider and got tipsy. Mr. Martin seemed sadly inadequate to history. Whenever we came by we would find him at his door, looking mild and affable and gray.

Though Mairs, the chicken man, had no alluring afflictions, he had a lovely skunk. The skunk was civil when we came to visit it, yet we watched it uncertainly. Its forbearance was hard to estimate, and as it lay all curled up in the shadow of its box, watching us too, there was something fearfully speculative in its gaze.

Mairs' interests finally covered more than skunks. Quantities of stylish cars began coming up the drive and vanishing behind the barns somewhere. They could only be bound for the brooder house—all come to visit Mairs. The traffic grew so thick that, though Mairs might be charming, he was not *that* charming, Father thought. And the visitors were found to be all stocking up on whiskey; those were Prohibition days. So Mairs, his still, and his happy clientele were banished. Terry and I were sorry.

The men who lived far from the farm ate their lunch in a

row on a bench in the carpenter shop. It was a broad work counter, built along a wall that they leaned against, their legs stretched out in front. Their faces and their shoulders and the bottoms of their boots extended in lines above my head, as I sat on the floor in front of them, wishing they would go.

We used to love the shop and were fair carpenters when the men were not there. But when they were, everything went wrong. A saw that had been docile would give a piercing shriek, shiver, and stop dead; or a board twice one's height that one had hauled to the vice would skid and slap the floor like an explosion. Something always called attention to us. It was dreadful; it meant the men would help. Somebody would clamber off the bench, and take over; the rest would stop their talk; and one stood feeling foolish, one's childish work revealed, waiting to say, "Thank you."

Saying thank you was a trial in itself. We knew the gap between things felt and said. Thanks were clearly insufficient if one was deeply pleased, and if not, they were silly. There was the question too of choosing the right moment to speak, and of speaking loud so people could hear. The process was a tiresome, uncomfortable feat, although a worthwhile present, or any other proper gain, compensated for the effort.

When I counted the people I knew for Teresa, Townsend was the most important on the farm. He was a person I thought of dramatically and gravely. His quiet face and manner attracted me always, but his particular significance had to do with my vivid recollection and my high respect for what became of him one day.

It was "dolls' day" on an August afternoon. The dolls were being read aloud to. Teresa and I were on the verandah, surrounded by them all. We chose a certain day every summer for their care and devoted every minute to it. We

~ 54 ~

With Terry in the kitchen garden.

took special pains with those we had neglected. We worked like fury. We took them for long rides in the boys' wooden wagon round the circle—the front drive was a big sloping O—and they bumped in the sun gaily. We fed them rare dainties: squashed rose petals, and clover, and rich mixtures of pebbles and cool mud. We sewed for them; we gave

them lessons; we mended and entertained them. We spoiled them thoroughly.

This day was unusually festive because several of the dolls had just come home; they were back from a fortnight in the hospital with new arms and legs. They had arrived that very morning in a big brown parcel Ogard had brought with the mail from town.

We were happy as we sat with our children around us, reading them fairy tales. On the north lot the men were pitching hay. The air smelled sweet with it.

Then one of the workmen came running up the road and went into the house. There were low conversations in the hall, and people going back and forth. The limousine came to the door. And by and by Mother came out. She got in the car and said something to Ogard, and they drove away.

Then they told us Townsend had been killed. He had been working with the men on the north lot, riding on the hayraker. It had a seat high up, and back of it a row of iron claws. The tongue, they said, had split all of a sudden and broken in two and scared the team of horses. The horses bolted then, and Townsend fell off backward from the high seat. The prongs swooped down to lift the hay, and one of them pierced his head. He died almost at once, just bled to death quietly there. They said his skull was thin.

He had lived off the place in a pretty little house on a country road, halfway to town. When we saw Mother start off in the car, she was going there to tell his wife that he was dead.

I am not sure that I ended with Townsend when I counted up the people that I knew, but I think I must have lost heart at that point in my work. His death was a sober and sickening fact. It was also deeply edifying. Granny and Uncle Henry had died, to be sure, and I felt important having known them, but Townsend had done more than that—he had "met with sudden death." "From battle, and murder," we prayed in church, "and *from sudden death*, Good Lord deliver us." To have known someone this had happened to was a grave mark of honor.

These were most of the maids and men at home I used to count. I think Terry will say, "Well done." Anyhow, I am grateful to our old, inconsequential pastime. It has helped keep clearly in my mind, I believe, not only this particular acquaintanceship, but a feeling that went with it and that comes back again, over, above and stronger than nostalgia. It is a happy sense of fondness, of mutual sufferance, of surety accepted, of goodwill; it is, I think, in aggregate, the very sense of fellowship.

★　★

Opposite: Bobbie reading.

The library
in town.

EARLY
DISCOVERIES

T o tell truly what it was to be a child, to be new and growing up and learning, one must pay sufficient heed to discoveries, I think, of all shapes and sizes. Most of those I still remember are about myself, of course, with whom I had to deal primarily and had trouble getting used to, and the rest concern a puzzling relationship with God, and with mankind in the world about me.

A foremost discovery was me—a person—on some cellar stairs in the house in town. It was about the third step up, I think, that I made it. That is to say that, abruptly, and for the first time, I came upon me and perceived me being.

I had been playing with the boxes in the box closet below and I was filled with the exhilaration of foreign places. There were pasteboard boxes by the dozen down there, piled high on dim shelves. The things that had been in them and the things one could make of them were equally exciting to consider; their clean-cut squares and oblongs cast a geometric spell, and they smelt like gingham. It was a fascinating place, far away and still; one's heart beat faster than it did upstairs. Altogether, the journey from beginning to end was one of promise and adventure.

So as I proceeded up the long flight home, my mind was still highly keyed. It was ready for new thoughts, and was suddenly vouchsafed one in these words: "Someday you will be twelve!" I had not really considered this before as part of my own future.

I was thinking, "How queer!" and feeling rather scared, yet as if it had to do with someone else, when the "you" of "you will be" changed all at once to "I," and then the future met the present. I knew acutely, stirringly, "I am now . . . I am here." It was a heady, extraordinary moment. I sensed clearly time ahead, and time at that instant, and me climbing by the staircase walls; I felt, accurately, where I was—with time and me progressing. There were steps under me and then world and then sky; there were rooms over me, and then sky forever. Twelve years old, where I was going, seemed to be inside my head, a sort of light, behind my forehead.

In total contrast was another discovery on another flight of stairs in town. This time I was on my way to bed, and I was absolutely miserable, for Teresa was not with me. She was still downstairs, and that was a shocking situation. Our bedtime had always been the same until that dreadful evening.

Bedtime had been worthwhile when Terry came too, for, dull as was the end in sight, the means were amusing. The trip upstairs together was a lively interlude of shared investigation and dawdling. We would stop on the landing first, to look out of the long window and see what was happening outside, to watch headlights lighting up the snow or black shadows walking; then go on our way again, dallying on every step, judiciously pressing each tread with our feet for squeaking, at the same time trailing speculative fingertips along the wall to feel its roughness. We would study the picture of a Japanese fish in a black narrow frame, and the long Japanese lady a few steps above it. She wore a gray kimono and a fat, high obi. Her face was buff, her mouth an O. Her hair, a series of black pompadours, looked full of knitting needles.

When we were near the top step we would stop to fit our eyes against the squares of lattice screening off the hall and look way down at the wide front door and the fireplace opposite. There were often pennies in the bowl upon the mantelpiece, "in case the postman needs them." Only sometimes there were not—I needed pennies too, and filched them shamelessly.

We generally sat down here and there along the way, to work on tacks that held the carpet fast. Some were loose, and, with spasmodic diligence, we managed to make them looser.

We made various descents to pick up what we dropped—things likes marbles, rolled away at different levels—and often found ourselves upon the landing again, where, granted the grace of grown-up inadvertence, we had time to ride, in turn, down a short banister that ended in a flat wooden swirl, like the top of a tall graceful stool, excellent for survey. About then it was wiser for the silent team to dash, two steps at a time, upstairs to bed.

But tonight the team had broken up. Tradition had been done away with. What once was shared is not the same alone; this in itself was dreary. But besides the end of sharing, there was for me a greater loss, whose significance I might have felt less keenly had custom not been so brusquely changed on what had seemed a usual evening.

Madame Michelot was on hand to send us to bed. She used to come and stay for lengthy periods, to read French with Mother and to keep us talking it. On Miss North's days off she took charge as governess. But in French or English, our routine remained the same.

Of course, Madame had said in the customary way, with customary dispatch, "*Il est sept heures.*" She may have added "Janet" instead of "*les enfants,*" but if so I did not notice.

I remember gathering numerous things to take upstairs and waiting by the bookcase with my armful, and thinking that Teresa was dangerously slow; she was at the desk, still scribbling. She had not even pushed her chair back in an on-the-way position, a pose that seemed to quiet older people, and, though Madame had not become vocally impatient, still she must be getting restive. I was anxious for

~ 62 ~

Teresa, and admiring too. I thought her very brave.

Then, to me, Madame exclaimed, "*Mais que fais-tu, mon petit chou?*"—we were always "little cabbages" to Madame—"*Va vite te coucher! Dépêche-toi donc, voyons!*"

I answered, naturally, "*J'attends Teresa.*"

And then I was given the wretched information that Terry would sit up later from then on. Teresa went to school, and on that day, it seems, she had first come back with homework. There was no use waiting any longer, Madame said. I must run along to bed immediately. She said it all in a reasonable, bright way, as if it were normal news.

I stood appalled. It had been my special ploy ever since I could remember to blind myself to what divided Terry and me. I had been remarkably proficient at this hopeful, hopeless game. The things Teresa did that I was not old enough to do nor unfortunately yet able to, were, although discouragingly clear, so familiar I overlooked them. In this way, I had accepted Terry at school. It was no surprise at all when she had to go. I carried on as always, weaving little square mats out of strips of colored paper for Miss North, and practicing my letters at the round oak table, toward the dollar Granny promised on writing one's name. Miss North had wisely made "pretending school" a kind of game. I remember cheerfully stamping through the day nursery door, shedding imaginary snow, beating cold hands, pulling off pretend galoshes, and hanging up a make-believe coat. My thoughts were proficiently directed. I maintained my self-esteem.

But that night I was caught unarmed. Equal bedtime was a symbol of our unity. Now, sent upstairs alone, my difference was exposed—I was only a little sister.

In that despairing moment my mind no doubt released much earlier disgrace and suffering, for a youngest child is special prey to sudden, sad abandonment. There is no one

Mother's portrait of
my grandfather over the
piano in the main
hall of the
house in town.

ever behind and always someone ahead, and the battle to keep up is pretty discouraging. Bigger and older and more beloved though one's sisters and brothers be, one can neither equal nor become them. One has, after all, been left behind right from the start.

There sat Teresa—working? I could not see her face, and there I stood . . . I felt the tears sting. Madame must surely know this could not be. I *must* stay up! I *must* keep up with Terry! She would not allow this brutal difference? She would let me be the same? I suppose I beseeched her. Plainly it did no good. All I recall is making my way to bed.

I took a few steps toward the doorway and waited. The tears splashed down my face. I clung to the day nursery threshold, but not a word was said. I crossed the hall slowly. "She'll call me back?"—but she did not. I started then up the long stairs.

I climbed them blindly, by lonely inches. "Oh please dear Lord, please make it not true!" I stopped . . . I gave it every chance to change. But nothing did, and I went on, up and up those endless steps, facing utter misery. The horrible discovery that what I dreaded most had happened was more than I could bear. They had pushed me back to being exactly what I feared: "too young," forever outcast.

Out of self-preservation I tried to tell myself we would do all else together, Terry and I, but I knew it was no good. It was useless to pretend. Here was manifest defeat.

Though my proper place in life, to me, meant Terry's place, it was in the sense of privilege and age. Otherwise I stayed where I belonged, contentedly enough. I had no wish to usurp Teresa's ways. I knew our natures were not just the same, and when I, in comparison, discovered myself wanting, this was food more for contemplation than shame.

Teresa's vigorous dealings with her own shortcomings

~ 66 ~

kept her busy. She was unremitting—a better man by far than I about trying to be good.

"DO ALL TO THE GLORY OF GOD; gave Janet cushion"— years later, Elleda found this in a desk written on the top left half of a white paper in Terry's schoolroom hand. The right half is headed, "TURN THY BACK AGAINST SATAN." Nothing more is noted there. Only a robin is standing in a corner far below. God's side has a bluejay. A vine, with colored balls swinging out of it, grows stoutly up the middle of the sheet. The designs are executed in blue and red and green, very neatly, with wax crayons.

This was Terry's most efficient moral stage, when she recorded her good and evil deeds, and decorated each edition conscientiously with flowers and growing things and suitable birds.

I have forgotten the high occasion of the cushion, but I recall a like report, except that God and Terry, and unfortunately Satan, had had a fuller day. The document, with lilies drawn around it like a frame, was crammed with accomplishment. I was with Granny, and I saw it. I was sitting on the floor in what was once the nursery but was now her sitting room. She was busy making lace, and I was watching the bobbins go, when Elleda, or Miss North, came in with the chronicle. Granny took it and read it through. She laughed a good deal. She said she would like to keep it, please.

I was filled with mild surprise, and a warm pride for Teresa, and a kind of sad acceptance about me. I thought it would be lovely if I also made a list. And I knew I never would. I wondered why, as I sat observing Granny fold the paper, and concluded that I lacked sufficient zeal. I cared, but not enough. It seemed too bad, but I accepted the discovery in the way that I accepted mediocre undertakings in other things. Terry's Easter cards, for instance, were much livelier than mine, her ideas more adventurous, like a

card that Mother kept: a brownie sitting on the Cross. Mine were orthodox and dull. Nobody saved them.

All this seemed right enough. But it gave me some concern to find how dull I was in more important ways; as when I found myself, to the best of my belief, gazing squarely at Our Lord. I saw Him in the sky one day, or thought I did, and I was shamefully inadequate.

I had been lying on my back on the warm summer grass looking at a kite that Ol was flying, when I noticed, beyond, across the west half of heaven, something bluer than the sky; the shape, whose proportions were perfectly distinct, of a person's head and shoulders. It was rather like the sculpture in the house in town mysteriously called "The Unknown Woman," only it was long, and squarer shouldered like a man, and not white, but still blue.

A bust of God? How foolish! More likely God Himself. For it did not stop, cut off, across the chest. It continued to the trees at the end of the sky. The trees screened the rest.

If this vision was an afterimage of the kite that I had gazed at until my eyes were stamped with it, or some other silhouette, a doll, a shrub, whose form remained, such pranks were still unknown to me. But I did consider other possibilities. It could not be a cloud, for whoever saw a blue one! and one that shape! and one that stayed stock still! And if it was not God, but someone else up there? No one else was apt to be so big, and besides, inhabitants of heaven should have wings—all but God. Thus I beheld Him.

Should I point Him out to Terry? She was helping Ol with the kite strings. I decided not to. I decided to think instead.

I lay a long time pondering. Was it possible that I was being singled out? Was this what people called a revelation? Would there be a message for me?

I waited with respect, but certainly no message came. It was more as if the Lord had stopped a moment at His window and was studying His world, and did not mind my seeing Him.

This was, I knew, a great experience in my life, a moment to be met with all my being. Yet something was not right; something in me did not work; I was not over-

Opposite: my brother Davidge.   ~ 69 ~

whelmed. I knew I ought to be, perhaps would be in a moment. But meanwhile, as I gazed at what seemed surely the Almighty, my thoughts remained disgracefully mundane. I felt no joy, no ecstasy, no love, no high connection. In fact, I only felt how impressive I should be, later, to other people.

I gather I was not, because the incident is closed firmly in my mind from that point on. I do not even remember who left first, the Good Lord or me.

But I found to my relief I was not always a dull witness. I thought I saw Him come to earth one day, no longer a blue giant, rather perhaps the Holy Ghost, as least *a* holy ghost. I was enchanted.

We had come out to the country on a cold Thanksgiving morning. The house was opened for that special feast, and I happened to be standing in the quiet living room when a shaft of light came through the doorway. It was the sun shining in, and the dust dancing. I had never noticed such a thing before. I drew my breath in quickly; it was such a lovely sight, slanting through the air, touching the floor. It was marvelous, and strange, and utterly beautiful. It made me feel the way I did sometimes in church, when I heard the soft chimes that Aunt Alicia had presented in memory of Uncle Henry after he died. They used to play them in the moment after the service of silent prayer, before one got up and gathered one's gloves to go. It was the same, only more intense.

I put my hand into that golden dancing air and felt it blessed. I was truly filled with wonder and delight. And even later when they told me the tiny stars were specks of dust, it did not hurt; I knew God had been there with them, a phantom thing, but much more real, more tender, more alive, than an image in the sky, which I could not love.

It was at special moments that one found God, single

moments independent of place and time, whereas, curiously, in the middle of religion one could lose Him altogether.

One discovered other things though, but mostly about people. At church I studied grown-ups and their ways: how some peeked when they were praying, just as I did; how the rector's wife was always late and came hustling up the aisle when the service had begun, which Mother said for rectors' wives was inexcusable; how little old Miss Pringle, whose wits were dim and who fortunately sat where we could see her, never put a penny in the plate when it was passed, but politely put her gloves in. My father, who generally received this offering, would gravely take them out and place them carefully beside her in the pew, while she watched him, beaming. Miss Pringle was delightful, but then she was daft.

I used to look the people over in the special way one can when one is not supposed to talk to anybody. I liked to see my father when he came back up the aisle with the others, carrying the collection; his white hair with tints reflected from the colored windows on it, his well-cut back, his formal coat. It was curious when a person was a part of life at home, to look on while he belonged to something else. It was as if he were himself, but in a frame, on view, but inaccessible.

As I sat there watching Father, I loved him so, it hurt. My heart was wrung with tenderness and pain. I used to wonder then, as I have wondered ever since, why it hurts so much to love. I thought forward, feeling sick, to the time that lay ahead when Father and Mother both would have to die. Could a person bear such loss? I knew with a faint heart this was something I would learn.

I loved my parents and revered them wholly. But the usual sort of grown-ups seemed absurd. The last thing one could wish for was to join that circumspect and dull, affected world one had to suffer, of people saying silly

things, and never climbing trees, or playing in a doll's house, or pretending. The most useless thing a wishful nurse could say to Terry or me was to ask us to behave like "little ladies." We greeted this with scorn and ribaldry. The idea was unthinkable.

In fact, our attitude toward grown-ups as a whole was definitely derisive and cynical. We saw through our elders more often than they knew, sometimes when they did not see through themselves. Each fresh discovery that they were not what they seemed diminished their status.

I recall a trying instance with Miss North. One day she found me reading Terry's diary. She made a righteous scene. She cried, "It isn't nice *at all* to look at anybody's private journal!" I was feeling grateful and surprised to see how honorable she could be about something that belonged to Terry or me, when she added, quite ingenuously it seemed, "Your own, you know, is full of careless spelling!" I thought of remonstrating and then I let it go. It was useless. It was typical.

A sorrier discovery was one I made in church: adults en masse were equally illogical. It was on a Sunday morning one winter of the war, when things had reached a deadlock in the trenches. Dr. Elliot was preaching a last sermon before he left to join the troops. He was speaking in a way that had taken my attention from making bunnies out of Mother's gloves; I remember watching him instead, and I remember really listening, until a vigorous statement gave me a pause. "We've *got* to win! *The Lord is on our side.*" I suppose it was the first time I had heard those words.

In spite of Mr. Raemaeker's cartoon of a "Sale Boche" standing on a pile of murdered children,one had the sense to know that all Germans were not bad, and that very likely most of them thought we were. To the Germans things would have to be the other way round. To them their cause was good. Terry and I had often wondered what they must

Opposite: Davidge, aged seven?   ~ 73 ~

think of us—that we were bad? It was almost certain.

Now it struck me that German priests, at that very moment, might be busy claiming God as partisan. They could stand, arms outstretched too, in exactly the same way, saying, "God is on our side."

We could not all count on the Lord to make us win. This was fallacy—but obviously happening! Each side simply believed, no matter what the enemy thought, that God was against the enemy. There was something deliberately wrong about all this, a sort of voluntary blindness in people, if they seriously thought the Lord would overlook the equal faith of other people.

I surveyed the adult world a little while with genuine interest, noting its unsoundness as complete, for even my own parents seemed part of this behavior. Grown-ups were made that way. I discussed it with Teresa for some time inside my head, I remember, as the sermon progressed, and I remember marking well what I was saying in anticipation of really saying it.

I had slight appreciation of the depth of real despair behind the seeming folly of grown-up views, for war, that war at least, was far removed for most American children. Terry and I, of course, had considerable plans, in case the Germans came; and though we shared in the amusement when our neighbor, Mr. Kirk, bought a donkey for his children to escape on, we hoped privately that the stalwart animal might play his noble role. We ourselves would elude the Boches on horseback. Only first we would cut off Teresa's plait. It was thick and hung a long way down her back and was, for me, a great convenience. It evened up the odds when we squabbled considerably, for though handicapped in size for wrestling, I could dart behind Teresa and grab the handy rope securely with both hands, and swing. We both felt, however, that something special should be done in the face of momentous calamity, and it seemed a fitting, satisfying thing to cut the braid straight off. Besides, the chance might never come again. We felt it must not be missed.

Yet there seemed little hope of personal danger three thousand miles away from the war itself. We were, in fact, gravely kept aware of how light our burden was; of how relatively little our country had to bear, having joined the fight so late; at what sacrifice of honor her delay, our parents felt, and at what cost to others. So when it was reported that our soldiers overseas were boasting they had come to win the war, and swaggering through lands that had given their life's blood, we were filled with hurt and shame. We were thankful Dav was there. We hoped everyone would meet him and soldiers like him, gentle, quiet men, "marching with the president to do their ver-r-y best," as in Harry Lauder's ballad.

Our apologetic feelings were somewhat relieved by a genuine right to personal anxiety. Alice was over there as well as Dav, and Ol would soon be going. One had reason therefore for legitimate concern, especially when Dav was sent to Flanders, and it was, for me at least, a comfort to have cause for just and serious worry.

But it was hard to live up to. For here again I made the sad discovery that I could not feel as deeply as I should. It was dreadful to have proved inadequate to God, the day Ol flew his kite, but this new deficiency seemed immeasurably worse—I was letting down my brother.

Every night I prayed that Dav would not be killed and tried to sense the danger he was in, to make the prayer a proper one so it would do some good, but every night I failed. I tried very hard to imagine war: the bullets; Dav wounded; Dav dead. I remember whispering, "He may be dying *now*" and waiting to comprehend it. But I only felt the dark, and my knees on the hard floor, and a hindering awareness of myself—the way I looked there, thinking.

But nothing ever troubled my formal prayers. These were purely automatic and a matter of speed, excepting the Lord's Prayer, where it suddenly came real, toward the end, with the welcome but puzzling reference to Elleda. For though no nurse was ever more adored, I was not clear why she was cosmically important. It was unexpected, too, where she came in: ". . . as we forgive those who trespass against us. *Elleda's not in temptation.*" But the Good Lord wished to know it then and there, and with ever recurring interest. I never got round to asking Elleda about it all; my curiosity was not immediate. Her condition seemed most fortunate, and it was nice she lived with us. I accepted the situation like most accustomed things as a matter of course. Still, it was curious.

Taking off with "Now I lay me," speeding to, and through, "Our Father," I would wind up in a hyphenated whirl, with: "God-bless-Father-and-Mother-brothers-and-sisters-friends-and-relations—AMEN!" That I liked. It was quick and sensible. I was not, to be sure, in full accord about relations, but supposed them better blessed.

I recited these learned-by-rote petitions Sunday evenings to my mother before clambering into bed, after she had read to us and taught us various things about the church, and Christ, and the early Christians. I remember a white light, and a hill, and a brown horse in a story about St. Paul, and my ill-concealed stumblings through the collect for the day, learned at a gulp on the way upstairs. Mercifully Teresa said it with me, speaking out in a firm enough way to disguise my mumble. But mostly I remember Mother sitting in a chair, and me upon my knees facing her lap, delivering a mechanical recitation to her skirt of my usual bedtime prayers. I never offered more, for it seemed a shameful thing to expose one's own endeavors to public view. So, when Mother used to say, a little sadly, "Janet, dear, don't you think that you could add a prayer for

Davidge?" I would mutter to her lap all I could honorably admit: "God bless Davidge," feeling sheepish as I did so. Only I knew my hard attempts to pray my best, and only I my failures.

I so often discovered the same shortcomings, the same apparent leanness of sensibilities, that, sitting once at my window, staring at the night, I decided I had no feelings. I remember wondering what it was going to be like, going through life that way. The future looked as dark as the night itself. I was alone, and troubled.

Yet my troubles were contradictory. I sometimes felt too much—and ignominiously showed what I was feeling. This was a deplorable discovery. I had all of the scorn and suspicion of a true New England child toward anything in the least demonstrative, and besides, everybody was expected not to cry on certain express occasions. Like when soldiers went to war and their families saw them off with a smile "although their hearts were bleeding." One must face up to the challenge like the posters and the songs—the way Peggy, a grown-up cousin, did beautifully. I heard someone telling Father how she sent her husband off, game to the end, blowing kisses.

But when I had said a last goodbye to Davidge at the station, I had not waved a gay farewell. I had started to, and turned back into the train. I was crying. I could not help it. I stood there, in the dingy narrow corridor, with my head thrown back to slow the tears, staring at the khaki ceiling, trapped—one who could not play the game.

Sometimes others played it queerly—like the telegraph official, vexed transmitter of salubrious morale, who had his own ideas about encouraging the troops—or else had had enough of it. Anyhow, before Dav left, he got an odd telegram from his godmother, Miss Willard, headmistress of a boarding school for girls. Every inch inspiring, apparently she had said: "When Duty whispers low, 'Thou

must,' the youth replies, 'I *can*.'" But when the message came, the youth had had a change of heart. Duty spoke and the youth replied, "I can't."

Even I could find this sort of thing refreshing. But my own incompetence had no light side. I continually found my own reactions to the world unsuitable and perverse.

~ 78 ~

My feelings about Zoë were wrong from the start. Zoë was my golden-brown dog, a gracious Russian wolfhound, intelligent, good, and beautiful—and my own. Ogard drove us to some kennels in the touring car one day, my father, my mother, Terry, and me. There I chose the gayest puppy, and by far the loveliest, among many brothers and sisters.

Everybody knew how glad I ought to be. I was keenly sensible of this myself, and glad I surely was to own this graceful creature, and greatly honored to take care of her. I taught her manners, and fed and combed and walked her, working earnestly at these daily tasks, yet something made me feel that I was somehow all along playing hostess to a young and elegant stranger.

She was a stranger to be proud of. I displayed her gratefully on Linden Street throughout the following winter. By accident my winter hat had quite a Russian look and went extremely well with a Russian dog. Moreover it was sherry-brown, exactly like my borzoi; my old suede coat was, too. We were mostly the same color and mostly the same shape, one long and up, one long and on all fours, and equally skinny. People said we looked alike. I quite agreed, and was glad they noticed. The likeness was, I felt, that of two aristocrats, with a suggestion of foreign background.

But at first this marked resemblance was all we shared. Our acquaintance stayed dishearteningly aloof. I was polite and so was she, but I was ill at ease and self-conscious when I talked to her, until a day that we were walking down a path in my aunt's garden when I suddenly gave up my stiff approach. I record unhappily the sickening baby talk that came like an inspiration. "Does oo want to come home now baby-dog?" I asked. She nuzzled her nose against my skirt. Her exquisite tail was wagging. She was quite as relieved as I. Our reserve had broken through.

From then on I spoke to her in this maudlin way, and it

~ 79 ~

seemed to set my feelings free. If I called her "doggie-woggie" my heart filled with a love I could not feel when I spoke sensibly.

Yet although this foolish jargon released my fondness for her, as playmates we stayed slightly artificial. Our friendship may have started out too carefully arranged. Or perhaps she was too beautiful.

When she died I was away at boarding school. I did not feel particularly bereaved. My roommate told me she was sorry with such warming sympathy I felt heartless by comparison.

When Granny died my behavior was outrageous. I was extremely disappointed in myself. My respect for the drama of heart-rending occasions made my conduct specially grievous. Elleda told us first, when Terry and I woke up, so we knew what had occurred in full detail. I was not personally affected. I liked Granny very much; I was used to seeing her at table and sometimes being with her in her sitting room in town, but I did not know her well. One heard charming things about her—that she was full of wit and moods—but I knew merely an old lady who dressed in graceful clothes, read us Dickens, made lace, and had lived in Italy. I was sorry she had died but I was not deeply hurt. The event of death itself, however, was shocking.

On my way downstairs to breakfast I was both excited and scared; I would soon be facing Mother. I wondered, tremulously, what I should find; I thought people changed at such enormous times. And then I saw her standing there, beyond the breakfast table, very quietly. I crossed the long room nervously to give my morning kiss. I felt conspicuous, foolish, and uncertain. I did not know if she would talk in ordinary words. Then I saw she had been crying. This was so unaccustomed that I felt almost ashamed. It seemed more like usual people than my mother. It seemed

~ 80 ~

to shrink her grief to a dimension I could grasp, and I found this embarrassing. And then speaking gently, she said our grandmother had died. I tried to listen suitably, but it is hard to bear, in public, the slow breaking of grave news, and if one knows it all beforehand, it may be quite unbearable. Excitement and self-consciousness had weakened my control. It broke. I gave an agitated giggle. A grin possessed me first, as I stood before her—and then the laugh. It was preposterous. No one paid me any heed, but the fact remained. I can still recall a feeling of appalled astonishment as I watched what I was doing. It was a mortifying revelation, and dreadfully discouraging. But a glad discovery was the clear, brave way that Mother made one feel about death and dying. She talked to Terry and me that morning, in the dining room. She made death on earth seem simply the other end of living, something plain, and right, and real; exactly as appropriate a happening as birth; as palpable, as true; something to accept, observe, and never run away from; a natural, important matter of fact. She did not mitigate the dreadful loneliness of those who loved the person who had died, but she showed us the world's unchanging government and made us look straight at the rules.

She rid us, too, of all fantastic notions about corpses, the superstitious and uneasy fears we might have learned from servants' eerie talk or made up in our heads. She pointed out that people sometimes acted rather strangely when a person in the house was dead. She said the maids might go about on tiptoe, for example, or whisper in the passage. She told us not to act in an unnatural way. There was no reason to. She said it sternly. The dead were only strange because one was not used to them. This was all that was extraordinary.

She told us Granny's body would be lying peacefully in her bedroom, where she died. The door was open and she hoped we would go in as often as we wished and stay there next to her, and pray, or take her hand. She made it seem a thoughtful, gracious visit.

Knowing what to do and how to feel was comforting. One was secure again and rather proud to share in this interesting thing, to be admitted to it. It was good to go by Granny's bedroom easily and know that one could enter when one chose. It looked a peaceful place beyond the angle of the door. But there were always people. I wanted to go in as Mother had suggested and stay with Granny for a little while, but privately, when no one was about to make me feel self-conscious. I wanted to be free to look at Granny very closely and see what she was like and if I minded. But principally I wished to say goodbye to her, in my own way, by myself.

At night, on the way to bed, I looked carefully around. There certainly was no one in the passage; nobody could see me and make me feel ashamed, as if I were doing something virtuous. Granny's door was still ajar, and as far as I could tell there was no one in her room then either. So I pushed the door a little wider open and stepped softly across the threshold.

The scene had the stillness of a painting, and the qualities of color and line as well. The slender form reclining there in absolute repose looked like Granny—but in a picture. Her white hair shone in the quiet light. She wore a purple dress, a rich and glowing shade; her hands, folded against it, were lucid ivory. There were soft white pillows behind her head and shoulders; they had ruffles that fell gracefully. She was lying on a couch. It was a deep and shadowy gray. Its half-back framed her profile darkly. The somber stuff intensified in a dramatic way her lambent pallor.

Death, in this silent room, was still and luminous, like a candle burning quietly. I was confronted by a marvelous serenity, separate and profound. I stayed, held motionless, for several seconds, and then the vibrant stillness relaxed its

~ 82 ~

hold. I approached the silent body to consider it carefully. Near to, the face was rather a horrid color. Yet it was beautiful, and since old age is pale, in death it was not startlingly different. Experimentally, I touched the pretty hair. It was wonderfully soft; I stroked it lightly. Then my fingers met the forehead. And something in me stopped— and fled. Death was ice cold.

For a moment panic seized me, but I stood my ground by forcibly reviewing what Mother had said. Here was death, and that was all; it was as it had to be; one must not run away from it. I pretended quite deliberately not to be afraid. And it worked. I was rewarded. Here was only Granny's body; it was cold and made of something more like soap than human flesh, because she had to leave it. And it was in our care; a poor deserted thing.

Before I left, I brushed my lips against her cheek, and the gesture was warm and spontaneous. I felt slightly conscious of doing the right thing and inevitably somewhat theatrical, but all that really mattered was, blessed happening, a feeling of utter tenderness. This was selfless and restoring, and a rich discovery.

I so rarely found myself behaving properly, feeling the way I thought I should, that a maxim I discovered somewhere about that time made up for a great deal. I heard with extraordinary interest one day the words "noblesse oblige."

Madame, in some complaining mood no doubt, was pointing out that people like my family, indisputably "noblesse," must not forget this precept. I asked her to explain to me exactly what it meant, and listened with tremendous satisfaction, interpreting the message as my rightful heritage, with all my soul and all my vanity.

We were walking in the country in the rain, climbing up the steep wood road, a road my mother painted at the time of autumn leaves, the trees golden, the road tawny. But when I see the painting, even now, the colors change. I am walking with Madame on a rainy day. The trees are silver-green on either side of us. The road is dark wet. I can still see distinctly how each footstep as I climb divides small pebbly streams, and how the tongues of my black rubber over-shoes push and curve against my socks. The white socks are soaked, spattered and transparent. They feel soggy and pleasantly lukewarm.

And I am thinking busily as I trudge along, weighing very carefully what has been said, secretly repeating "noblesse oblige" as mine; happy that I belong to it. I am perfectly aware that Madame, herself, has been speaking for a good French reason, but that is nothing—I have discovered an ideal that is both praise and challenge. Splashing through the puddles so many years away, I assume again the flattering cares of privilege. My spirit soars remembering the sodden, dripping trees. My shoulders square. I am ready for high endeavor. I am thinking with conviction and delight, "This is my code!" I feel absolutely splendid.

At that time I had some reason to feel as I did. I had recently discovered a magnificent fact. I did not tell Madame—one does not boast about these things!—but there it was. I had royal blood in me. I wondered if Madame could apprehend, however feebly, some lurking evidence of the royal strain. Did I show, somewhere about me, ineradicable marks of one descended from King Alfred? "On Granny's mother's side *straight back*," Teresa had explained, after talking once to Mother about the family. The likelihood that Mother had not meant the actual king never, happily, occurred to me. Straight to the king himself was where I wished to go—and there I went, delighted.

I had always loved King Alfred, and his cakes, and his appearances in and out of forests. Had I been asked to choose a king to be descended from, I could not have found a better one. The burning cakes, the ancient trees, the Robin Hood sovereign were a living part of history in my heart. That this heroic monarch was responsible for me was more than I could ask for.

I remember, during that walk with Madame Michelot, looking curiously at the veins that crossed my hands and wondering if a few drops of his blood at that moment were traveling through them. I wanted to deserve them, and it seemed a heaven-sent thing to find a motto both appropriate and challenging.

I rather doubt that my moral conduct suffered change. My obligations were not sufficiently spectacular, and the injunction was too grand. But one memorable day I discovered something directly helpful.

If we went into the town for any reason, in the summer, we came home again with Father, late in the day. One had to wait with Ogard in the car, outside the office, for what seemed like the entire afternoon, till impatience finally rose to an excruciating pitch, and the smell of city heat became quite sickening; or else one had instructions to go straight inside to Father, in his big private room in the west wing.

Having finally reached the door of a sort of antechamber, one pushed against it boldly and went in. Some person at a desk would cope with the event by summoning Mr. Poole, Father's secretary, a busy little man who looked just like a monkey, Mother said. As Mr. Poole always knew what Father wanted done with us, the person at the desk would resume his work.

I suppose one waited there if Father was busy and sat timidly on the nearest chair, but the memory is blurred. I can only see myself walking past the man at the desk, toward voices. I remember the open doorway and the room beyond, and the different height one saw things from when one was little, and the general scene before me: dark trousers stood about; I was conscious, too, of hands and the bottoms of waistcoats. Then I noticed faces; I remember them last. Some of them, after a second, looked familiar.

"Hello, Chickie!" Father would say, slightly surprised, as if he had forgotten I was coming. "I'll be ready pretty soon." And there I stood, while the faces all looked down with awful attention. And there I waited, out of place, while conversation was resumed and continued, for ten or twenty minutes.

I liked the room itself at other times: the dark chairs, the feeling of space, the airy windows; Mother's portrait of my grandfather above the mantelpiece, writing, with books beside him. Above all I liked the magic of Father's desk. On it was a button one pushed . . . and the door closed quietly. For Father never liked to cross a room and shut a door while someone was talking to him. I remember his explaining that it was often left ajar by mistake and—if people wanted to talk privately—he had to get up and close it—till he found this lovely way to make it shut itself.

But none of this made up for the frightful undertaking of coming alone to meet him there. It was almost impossible to face, until that special day.

I had got into the building as far as the marble stairs that rose spaciously up half the wall ahead. I observed the way they turned and climbed slowly out of sight . . . nearer the place I dreaded. I wanted wildly to run away, but I knew that would not do. I stood hovering and looked at the tall window framing the pale north sky. And then, against the light, at the bottom of the pane, I saw some lettering: "Go forward without fear and with a manly heart," I read; and underneath it, "Abraham Lincoln."

I remember thinking that my father must himself have had this put there at the time the glass was made, and feeling that, although my heart could never be a man's, the message seemed to be there for my benefit. It was as if it had been waiting till I discovered it. After that I managed to stay the course and went straight on, frightened still, but the master of my fear, sturdily up the stairway.

Since most of childhood has to do with finding out, there is no handy ending to early discoveries. They come continually to mind, most of them unforeseen, all of them wanting attention. But now that they have led me up a flight of steps again, close, in a sense, to where I started, on a cellar stair encountering myself, I find contained within that circuit what seem the most important ones—at least the first to come and the most persistent.

Bobbie and Terry?

WNO TRUCKITH INNOCENCE

I could never see why innocence was good. Innocence and ignorance were synonymous to me, and the words "an innocent child" were personally insulting, stupid and ridiculous. I was annoyed by their assumption and uncomfortable for the grown-ups who used them and exposed how little they knew. It was they who were innocent, poor things. Even the rector preached a sermon on the Innocence of Children one Sunday as a fact—and one to be recommended. Unquestioning belief in such a state was certainly stupid; bland approval seemed downright irresponsible. Still, there it was! To every grown-up innocence was good, and attributable to children, willy-nilly.

When first encountered it seemed a limited sort of virtue devoted to storks who carried babies out of the blue, or, in European countries, to cabbages and mushrooms under which babies, clearly dwarfed, were found. It was innocent to believe in stories like that. I was glad nothing so foolish applied to me.

Myself, I knew most satisfactorily how babies came. One woke up and found a baby there beside one. God had put it on the pillow in the middle of the night. That was all. It was His gift.

I can still see the picture I had in my mind: a young woman with brown hair, in the rose guest-room bed, with a shadowy kind of baby on the pillow at her left, and the fine lace bedspread Granny had made flung over her. She was no one I knew, nor was the baby. I had no personal connection with either one. I think the reason I recall the scene so vividly may be that it stood for sufficient knowledge.

It was at least a step in the right direction. Someone I consulted must have tried to set me straight in a slight way, and I supplied the rest. I felt wholly adequate. It was excellent to be wise, to have no truck with innocence.

But wisdom was demanding, and I soon learned that there was more to having babies than I thought; there was the jump from being given one to the odd way they began; sex reared its challenging head. Yet I managed to hold my own, to my own mind at least, and at every stage of learning I was happily convinced I knew almost everything that I was not supposed to.

As youngest child, my position was fairly strong. I had access to information in advance. I shared at once whatever Terry gleaned, and we both learned much from Bobbie. She was an excellent eldest sister, technically grown up,

Above: still life.   ~ 89 ~

even married, yet we considered her our equal.

When I was seven she had a baby, to our welcome enlightenment. She told us many things we wished to know. I remember a discussion once about the whole event, in the Big Room at Chatham. Bobbie was at Mother's desk, trying to write something and getting nowhere because Terry and I were there. I remember asking questions and listening carefully as I balanced over a Windsor chair from the back rung. The most fascinating part was splendidly funny—realizing out of where a baby came. I knew by that time where it stayed till it was ready to be born, but was vague about its exit. That it then appeared head first out of such a ridiculous place was a remarkable arrangement. It was actually true though! A fact to be believed! I remember laughing merrily—and, along with laughing, taking the idea into my head and thinking, "This needs getting used to."

The notion must have settled fairly comfortably, however. I do not remember giving it much heed except for wondering a little about our neighbor, Mrs. Kirk, a lady of vast gentility who had had two strapping daughters. It seemed incredible. Even Mother thought it odd, I discovered later. She said once with a chuckle, "I always wonder how the Kirks ever managed to have two children." I was older then, of course, and I remember feeling pleased at being spoken to almost like a grown-up, and I remember hoping she had really noticed who I was, or if not that nothing would remind her.

One felt curiously responsible for what older people said and conscious that it might be a mistake, that they might have quite forgotten they were talking to a child, and would suddenly remember. I endeavored to protect them, and tried to respond to the even slightly daring from my elders so that nobody would notice any silly self-consciousness which might point to my age. The slightest indication of surprise of course was fatal; I had to try to laugh in a natural way with just enough approval to fill a person's place effectually, without being noticeably present.

With contemporaries it was usually the other way round, above all if someone told a daring joke. Not many children knew any but sometimes someone told the clumsy kind of story that youngsters start with, always recklessly far-fetched, generally handed down at school by the few biologically well informed. I had to live up to this, and therefore act almost exactly as I tried not to with a grown-up. For, though it was important to cover up surprise, approval should be hearty and conspicuous. I laughed extra hard and extra long to show I was no prude, and to show I got the point—if by luck I did. If I did not, I laughed even louder, approaching hysteria, trying wildly to conceal the alarm inside. And someone usually sensed it, with the clairvoyance of a horse, and had the same horrid impulse to make the most of it. The unseating cry would come, "She doesn't see the point!"

"Of course I do!" I countered. "Don't be silly!"

I generally managed to keep up my reputation by looking as if I knew more than I did. But whatever the result, dread of losing face was such that even now I am stricken with the memory of panic sometimes at the approach of a dirty joke—the same beginner's worry that I may not understand and shall have to endure pretending to.

With close friends being stupid about jokes was all right, of course, and consolingly reciprocal. I could talk about anything I wanted to with them without feeling shy or foolish. In fact, it seemed essential to, in order to compare things—all things—and think them out that way. It made the most of thinking, just as sharing what one did made the most of doing, at least for me.

I used to wonder how single children lived; once I tried to

picture what it would be like. I was going through the pantry at Chatham at that moment, and I stopped to think about it. I must have been quite young, because I tried to imagine being bathed alone, without Teresa. The thought of having nobody to play with in the tub—to sail the little boats and the celluloid fishes—desolated me. I pushed the thought away quickly and retreated. But another idea followed, and it was worse. If doing things alone was hard to contemplate, thinking things alone was inconceivable. With no collaborator, no comrade to conjecture and decide with, one would barely be alive. I had a frightening suspicion I would as good as disappear without Terry as my identity. I remember a flattening moment of fear, and then letting the truth console me. I was reverently grateful that Teresa and I were together in a big, happy family. I remember looking through the window and into the sky, where God was taking care of things, and saying, "Thank you."

Without Teresa I would indeed have been diminished, at least so far as knowledge was concerned. As to figuring things out to combat innocence, my shameful ignorance would have been pitiful.

There was always more to learn to keep up one's good name. I forget the right order chronologically, but I remember certain stages where I know my knowledge stopped. For instance, about babies. When contemplating Mrs. Kirk giving birth to hers, I certainly never guessed how they began. It was hard enough to imagine their prim mamma in the unlikely role of bearing them. Had someone told me then that babies had to be begotten, and by a man, and how, it would have seemed crazy—and trying to envisage her stout spouse in such a part would have been plain impossible. It was preposterous to think of him without solid clothes or in bed—let alone in bed with a lady!

I discovered what made fathers by degrees too slow, or vague, to be recallable. What I remember, once I knew, is how curious it was that it could be accomplished civilly. It was hard to understand how a practicing father could be one with any sort of dignity, and harder to relate the situation as a whole to sentimental, romantic love. Cupids, orange blossoms, delicate blushing maidens, and suitors proposing timidly appeared as foreign to its impudent requirements as did proper respectability. Clearly everyone must suffer a breathtaking change. Furthermore, everyone must know it, about himself and everyone else, which was really very funny when one watched people talking politely. Yet they seemed to set great store by the whole affair, well over and beyond the line of duty, so I tried to find out why, and above all to figure out exactly how they went about it.

There were poses to consider, no matter how strange. Things like squatting, the way my uncle's silhouette did while my little cousin happened to be awake one night and watched it from her cot. She was sleeping in her parents' room for some forgotten reason—the nursery quarantined perhaps, or freshly painted. Anyhow, all at once, she perceived the curious image dimly visible in the dark. It stayed profiled against the lightly curtained windows for a second. Then it sank, and disappeared. She was very young indeed then, but the scene came back to mind when she and Terry and I and her little sister were strolling through their dining room one day a few years later, discussing sex intently. We stopped a moment there, and pulled some chairs out from the table and sat down, the better to attend, while she told what she had seen, and then laughed a little shyly and said, "That might be what was happening." We all felt a bit dismayed envisioning my uncle, as if we were being rude to him and my aunt; but we saw no other reason for such a stance in bed, and agreed sex had to do with it.

A further clue confirmed this. I picked it up one day, perforce, from a girl at school. I could probably have gotten all kinds of information from her, but she was different from us for that very reason, so that one felt uncomfortable and eschewed her confidences. That day, however, she cornered me.

"Do you know the definition of a gentleman?" she said. "A gentleman's a man who leans on his elbows!"

There at least was a useful hint. A gentleman on his elbows, the rest of him prone—on a sled for instance— would undoubtedly have squatted on his way to that position, much like my uncle in bed. But his lady? Aunt Amy? I pictured a long silent shadow, and left her at that.

Getting married must be singularly embarrassing at first. Did people know what to do? Did they need directions? I tried often to conjecture how they met the new condition, what they felt, what they said—if they spoke at all. Most novels told a lot about falling in love. One could study what people said and their general behavior. But novelists were circumspect in those well-mannered days, and the facts of sex were discreetly avoided; they usually came to pass after the ending of the book in any case, since it was not till then that whatever kept the hero and the heroine apart was overcome, and they could marry.

If I liked the story, though, I made up more of it myself and often ran straight into the situation. I still remember all except the actual dialogue of a bedroom scene I worked on diligently. I was adding to the plot of a story I had loved about a favorite hero and heroine. It had become their wedding night, and I was trying to sustain a high mood of delight and wonder.

I got them to their room with light banter and stirring looks. And the bridegroom closed the door. And they stood there smiling . . . I wondered if perhaps he should undress the bride a bit, but that led, I thought, to difficulties. So they took their own things off, with a little gay discourse, and once he stopped to kiss her gleaming shoul-

der, and she stood a minute blushing before undoing something else—that was a lovely sequence! I had him turn his
back to take pajamas from a suitcase after that, so she could
slip into a nightgown, and he would not see her naked till
the proper time arrived to have him totally overcome. I had
a little trouble with ordinary events, like when they
brushed their teeth and washed their faces, but on the whole
the scene went on, successful as could be, till they were
ready to get into bed. Then I wondered whether or not they
would say their prayers, and whether they could without
appearing righteous. They might be shy about it. Nevertheless, I knelt them down for just a second and bent their
heads. And at that point I left them; I suddenly felt tired at
the thought of having to get them into bed. The transition
was too much, and I felt quite unequal to their future once
bedded, so I gave up. I recall a pleasant feeling of progress
achieved, though. I had made it possible, so far as it went.

From a different point of view, it was equally rewarding
to make up stories about myself, and easier. There were
no uncertainties, like guessing about grown-ups, no
anachronisms like making love. I was always my own age;
all I wanted from my hero was admiring attention, which I
managed to gain. A "hero" to Terry and me meant a
distinguished-looking man who was "deep—with a sense
of humor." It was delightful to communicate with him at
will, in full control of the situation, behaving charmingly.
    The best place to make up stories was riding in the car on
long journeys when talk had ceased. In those days open
touring cars had sideseats like some taxis, but facing forward. That was where we liked to be. We felt tied down in
mind and limb between two grown-ups in the back, where
they sometimes stationed one of us. The seats were hard,
but our arms were free, and our feet independent, and our
thoughts were too; people rarely interfered. I sat contented-

ly for miles, alert with make-believe, being witty and attractive or exceedingly brave in some splendid situation miles away from the traveling car and the winding Connecticut road. I gazed absently, as the highway bent, dividing the woods and fields; gazed vaguely on past Ogard's head—save a time when the scene was different: another head was there instead, and the highway was in England.

But that countryside was more than a vague accompaniment to make-believe. It was a live accomplice. The road was a "gypsy's ribbon"; Shelley's skylark soared; a rabbit hustled by consulting his watch. Fiction and reality were inextricably twined, even as past and present.

And the present was overwhelming—England was full of heroes. I remember one well in the yard of a country pub—tall, good-looking, lean, in a grayish Burberry—who stopped a moment near me, arranged the belt of his coat, got into a small two-seater, and drove away. Conceivably one might encounter somebody like that again, and attain his notice. . . .

I conjured meetings with all sorts of handsome Englishmen, observed and overheard with recognition because they lived up so exactly to what I had foreseen as a result of plays and fiction. I set to work expectantly on likely scenes each morning in the car, as soon as we started off and I was well settled in on my allotted sideseat, where I could think undisturbed. Terry was on the other one similarly engaged. I remember clearly how she looked once. She was grinning cheerfully, staring vaguely ahead. Her lips were moving as if she were thinking words, but so imperceptibly that only I would notice. I laughed; we were both so busy.

I myself had just run into the Prince of Wales. I had wandered down a lane—and there he was. By some wonderfully good luck he was going for a stroll. I rose to the occasion magnificently. I said something light and funny, which made him laugh. We started talking then, easily.

And since in these adventures people naturally found me an exceptionally interesting girl, memorable, in fact, to the discerning, with a face artists would like to paint, the Prince was no exception. In fact the theme progressed till we were dancing at a country house party.

But what was singularly important about the whole thing was that the Prince accepted me as valid. Whoever they might be, my English heroes found that, like themselves, I was a chip off the old block, for my stories invariably stressed my cherished connection. I felt deeply about England. I always had. Father used to speak of it sometimes as "that wonderful little island," and my heart would leap. Always I was grateful to be one of its descendants; I felt very near of kin, the three centuries between me and my ancestors who had left it seeming of little consequence.

Driving through England, therefore, at fourteen, I made up my happiest stories. The only interruptions, other than talk, were flapping maps that Father handed us intermittently. Like most men, he loved a map. I hated the dead things and did not care where we were in print. Besides, to hold one's eyes onto joggling names for long made one feel hot and like kicking. I remember the blessed moment of relief when at last I could return to my own adventures.

But they were wholly romance. Their connection with sex was slight and purely sentimental. In real life, at the opposite end of the pole, sex as research continued. My knowledge grew slowly, through hearsay, print, and a process of gradual absorption.

Each new idea, or often an idea already old, kept finding its own place and settling in. I remember once remarking the procedure in myself while it was going on. I had been studying a picture in a history book at school of a statue, a young Greek with obvious genitals. I had never come across what was so plainly not a fig leaf before, and I was surprised. Details were hard to see in the flat, gray print, but I discerned the general pattern clearly, and later, when its image kept on coming back to mind, I noted patiently that it had to; here was one more unexpected thing which had to find a place in its own time as an idea to be accepted—like bosoms. They surprised me too when I thought of them one day, quite suddenly, as separate entities and not as mere familiar bulges in women's shapes. They had had to be gotten used to. I remember walking slowly through the schoolhouse hall, wondering what my next preoccupation would be.

I think these concepts took their time mainly in order to be real, and not because I found them uncongenial. Almost nothing I discovered about sex when I was little seemed at all displeasing.

At times the effort to find out things became trying. I disliked the work of looking up words, yet the dictionary offered scraps of scattered information if I persisted doggedly. Most words were boomerangs and described a useless circle—like *womb* to *uterus* to *womb*—but there was always a slight chance of finding something promising that would lead to something new. So in the line of duty, I followed every clue up and down the closely printed columns, lifting and pushing over heavy blocks of pages in the tome on a stand in the library. I used to take my place before it, having come into the room at a moment when conditions were favorable, and Mother was not at her desk, or anyone around to ask what word I wanted. But while my eyes were searching, I was listening to the hall and the staircase that went up to Mother's winter studio. I felt guilty, and hurried, and ready to run away; and my stomach felt uncomfortable and fluttery.

I remember another uncomfortable condition. It lasted through most of a summer—a state of long waiting for Mother to say she would like to have a talk with me. She had had a talk with Terry, at about my age, explaining

~ 98 ~

about sex and growing up to it. So now the prospect was that she would have a talk with me of exactly the same sort.

It was a mortifying outlook. Sex was not a topic one should talk about with Mother. No true grown-up really liked to mention it, which was awkward in itself, but I knew well, through Teresa, that this was worse—this was sex and *me*! To be officially involved in that questionable subject was what made it so distressing. My pride and sense of decorum were equally offended. I tried to delay the indignity and ran away from Mother, prudishly, all summer, never daring to be alone with her.

It was a nerve-racking time of never feeling safe. I tried to keep in fairly hidden places in case she happened to go by. The most chancy one—my favorite when I had a book to read—was the verandah. It ran east to north to west; one could face three different ways. I chose what seemed the safest. But always I felt too exposed, and much too alert to pay sensible attention to the story I was trying to read.

I was not alert enough. I have forgotten which direction Mother came from in the end, but I remember her standing there before me. I was curled up on a hammock, and I looked up from my book—and I remember staring, and the way my blood slowed down as she greeted me lightly. She asked what I was reading, I think, as she sometimes did when she saw me setting forth with a book from the grown-up bookshelves. Once she stopped me reading something because I was too young; I do not remember what, but I felt shamefaced, and the next time she enquired, I was full of misgivings about *The Lonely Lady of Grosvenor Square*. Yet when I showed it to her hesitatingly, she said it was a charming story, and I was filled with pride at my own good taste and delighted to see she was pleased. Those were chance encounters, though. Mother never sought us out to see what we were reading or doing. Yet now she had come. It was horribly clear that this was the moment I dreaded.

But it was not at all dreadful. It was a pleasant conversation on a lovely summer's afternoon. I remember Mother sitting beside me on the hammock and, far away, the misty hills, and the green sweep of lawn, and the smell of hot paint where the sun crossed the verandah. I remember the slow summer sounds as well, and Mother talking quietly, and my thinking how easy it was being after all, and looking straight at her, and paying attention.

She talked about the way a human being started. I considered the wonderful, quick chemistry. She told me precisely what nature intended of me. It was interesting. Then it was ended. My relief was overwhelming, and I think, from then on, I felt—as a person—more authentic.

But still I was no clearer about the etiquette of mating. I could not think how people would behave, till Terry found a book on the detective-story shelf, on army hygiene as I recall. (Army seems odd, though, for apart from frightful ailments with beautiful Greek names, what I remember of the book is wholly unmilitary. We must have read another one, I think, at the same time.) Anyhow, what we found was excellent. It was a painstaking account on the subject that we wanted—a whole chapter about "Sexual Intercourse," written for the "guidance" of the newly married husband. We were delighted and learned a good deal.

I have forgotten most of it, except that ladies should have husbands who were—I think the phrase was—"mindful of their needs." And one outstanding need was fruit. A mindful husband would provide it, and he was right: it was pretty essential in order to save the situation when he went straight off to sleep the very instant his work was done. A husband dropped right off, it seemed, without a word of warning. He had to. The exertion was terrific. But this tended to make a woman feel left out, the author said, so a bowl of fruit was recommended. From that day on, I pictured deserted wedded ladies munching apples late into the night. It seemed a placid, even a boring, solace, and yet important. I respected it.

For even that homely scene managed somehow to suggest an aftermath to something rare and strange; the same thing that fiction decorously implied—or by that time frankly acknowledged, the war having made short shrift of prudery, so that sex was openly discussed in reputable novels, to be found like any others at large on a living-room table. One of these I read because a real British major, staying with us once in the country, and just out of the trenches, told Mother in my hearing that it was good, and remarkably true. In this I came upon a scene where a soldier and a woman lay together in the midst of grief and bombs and forgot all about them for the whole time they were mating. The act of sex was clearly enthralling.

We wondered how long it took. It was important to discover in order to understand correctly. But since time was never mentioned, we never could decide whether it lasted for a second or for hours. What was increasingly apparent was that people loved to mate, for their own sakes, apart from having babies, and that people were impelled to, anyhow, by passion—a fascinating instinct.

It did not depend on love; and it was worse for men. It could possess a man alone with a pretty girl, particularly at night, because of association. It was especially roused by virgins. An honorable man who happened to be in love with the virgin he was with was in a dilemma. He underwent a frightful struggle between his noblest feelings and mounting passion. It took heroic self-control for nobility to win. The battle was pretty exciting. I was glad to belong to the sex that could occasion such a stirring combination of wildness and chivalry.

But I rather looked down on the weakness of a species that went easily out of control, a control, furthermore, that seemed to depend largely on feminine behavior and whim.

This assumption was supported, I remember, by a cousin whose mother had once explained that a girl was unkind who allowed young men to kiss her, because it made them "passionate," and then they would be left in fevers of desire and would lie awake all night, or—I forget whether she told me or if I myself concluded—even end up with a prostitute. Although I knew this cousin slightly, and condemned her because I had once heard her speak of her "opinion," a pretension that in someone my own age I considered sheer effrontery, I was interested this time, and shared her attitude of enlightened understanding. I remember thinking also that kindness to young men, in my own life and hers, seemed madly previous, but I felt as superior as she did to their weakness, and saw a need to be philanthropic.

If more arduous for males, passion seemed nevertheless to be fairly dependable and clear for them. Plots hinged predictably upon it in novels new and old, whereas the evidence about its conduct in females disagreed, or was sometimes wrong and confusing.

When the great Victorian novels were our most important books, we spent a lot of time with the nineteenth century, where allusions to all intimate activities, though vague, and circumspect, and sentimental, were nonetheless apparent—it did not befit a lady to be anything but condescending, tolerating scandalous behavior in the dark in exchange for having babies. It was not easy to get rid of this idea when, later, we discovered its reversal in our own times. We approved of women being just as passionate as men and demanded their full right to be, wholeheartedly, yet it seemed a risky thing if they gave up secure detachment for undefended sharing. What if passion, once exposed, was not altogether shared? Was even greeted by surprise? Or indulgence? Our encounters with Victorian belief made such ideas alarming. However, if a lady was sufficiently adored, there was no valid reason for concern.

Mother's studio in town.

Then even the very proudest could abandon herself to passion unrestrainedly.

At what point this should be, Teresa and I discussed with

practical attention, since with reasonable luck we ourselves would one day be involved. There was a moment in *The Sheik*, that daring best-seller—bound, I remember, in suitable scarlet—which was exciting about it. I came upon the passage in the studio, during a rest from posing.

We were often Mother's models, especially in summer, for ten cents an hour, from nine till one. The hours sometimes dragged; it could seem ages until lunch, staring into space and not wiggling. Yet we seldom really minded; it was often interesting, and there were many pleasant things about the studio.

One simply sat there, alone and abstract upon the platform, surrounded by the quiet a room contains when thoughtful work is going on; a quiet which is live, and unhurried, and unlimited. Or one listened while Miss North read out loud, which she did well. Or one enjoyed engaging bits of conversation which broke the silence off and on when Lady Jo was there, Mother's closest friend, another artist.

Bobbie had raised her to the peerage when she was little. I suppose she heard the grown-ups saying, "Jo," and supplied the gentle prefix, descriptively I think; Lady Jo was a charming lady. When she was painting too, and one sat on the small stage, present yet removed, it was fun to listen. Long intervals of work would be broken by a chuckle and a lightly irreverent remark, or sometimes by a critical or speculative comment, interesting to ponder and illuminating. One sensed the many years they had worked and laughed together, and the goal they shared in tackling a new task, and one was conscious of the wonderful repose between old friends, the respect and perfect candor.

I last remember Lady Jo after Mother died. She came up from New York the day of the funeral. It was good to have her with us. She looked consolingly unchanged, only very, very sad.

We met her in the hall.
"Where is she?" she said.
Above: mother's painting of me.

Teresa indicated the library.

She turned away and walked slowly to the coffin and stood there a long time.

But in my childhood days, when she was part of every summer, I remember her mostly in the studio. It was Lady Jo, with Mother, who released me "for ten minutes," when I retired with *The Sheik*. I had been staring fixedly at a little six-inch statue of a bronze Egyptian god, which I had to hold upright on the arm of my chair, so near my eyes that I saw him double. I wondered if my eyesight had gone wrong and decided it was better not to mention it.

It was a welcome change to curl up on the wide sofa and return to my desert romance; and splendid when the sheik took the reluctant English lady in his arms and kissed her fervently. At first she resisted. Then the thrilling moment came—all of a sudden, she *responded*! I recall the swift rapture that ran though me as I read in the even light of the studio window.

But why did she choose that particular instant? How soon should a person give in? There was no way of telling, even in *The Sheik*. It remained a knotty problem.

I used to wonder if I was passionate myself. I was "sensuous," I found, when I learned the word, and there seemed a slight connection between them, although to be sensuous was wholly earthbound, an animal enjoyment of the colors and the textures of lovely things like tortoiseshell and peaches. In a way it was all right, because Keats was sensuous too, especially in comparison to Shelley, who was shining and soared high. Keats was vivid from the ground, with earthly things, though beautiful. But I was not a poet. My own sensuousness seemed disquieting rather than beautiful. I responded to the softness of velvet, mere cloth, with such relish that it rather worried me.

Then Terry and I discovered I was passionate, too. This was as it should be, and interesting. We read in Scott

Fitzgerald about a girl who was, very. There was a special way to tell. A "revealing white line" ran across her upper lip. We studied our own lips instantly. I forget if Terry found one; my eyes were glued on me, and I did, quite indisputably. To be so obviously branded was abashing, we agreed; substantiated passion was somewhat sobering. At least, thinking it all over one winter's night in bed, I can still remember wondering, what with being sensuous, too, how I would probably turn out—whether I was apt to be a streetwalker. I recalled a dire description in a poem of Oscar Wilde's of a painted face at night beneath a streetlamp, a deplorable place to be, all alone, and bad. Yet there was that possibility.

I pictured prostitutes in several different ways. They seemed more or less symbolic and slightly biblical when their daytime lives were mentioned and they were individual people. Nocturnal ones were nameless. The face beneath the streetlamp moved in and out of doorways with silent escorts. Then, again by day, nameless still, but in collection, they turned into clinical problems supplied by *Army Hygiene*.

That useful book, and others we discovered of its kind, made us quite as well aware as Miss North of why she hustled us away from a matinée we got to once by mistake, in Washington. It was a mortifying exit from the second or third row right after the first-act curtain. Before anyone else had risen we were walking up the aisle, with our hats and coats on, beside our governess.

We were in Washington for Easter. Our parents had brought us with Dav and Ol, and Miss North, to see that lovely city, and we had all gone to the theatre, but that was Shakespeare, with Southern and Marlowe. Only Terry and I were taken to this other, unknown drama, which turned out not at all what it had seemed; we were definitely misfits for everyone to see. I was twelve then, and Terry fifteen.

The play was called *The Aftermath*; it was the aftermath of war. The hero had returned from overseas. He looked a normal person, but there was something wrong about him. He had headaches, and they were worsening. He told a doctor, who I think had come to dinner, all about them. The doctor asked him questions more and more gravely, and traced him back to France again, and there, regretfully, to a cocotte—which was pretty ominous. I had a feeling of fluttering confusion for Miss North as the awful consequences dawned upon me; otherwise, I felt content at apprehending how, in time, his fingers would fall off, and his brain start rotting. At the end of the first act, the curtain fell just after the doctor had pronounced the dread word: *syphilis*.

Miss North by then was sitting on the edge of her seat, explaining in a troubled whisper this was not the sort of play Mother and Father had foreseen. We would leave at once. And she removed us.

It was a pleasure, nevertheless, to know why we were removed, to understand from what we were being saved, and to be successfully past saving, a condition that allowed us to tolerate even Miss North.

In addition to contending with the innocence of children, one had also to combat its grown-up relatives. For instance, I remember when the "double standard" hit me, somewhere along the way. Miss North tried to explain it. I was privately astounded and resolved to put my foot down firmly.

I looked into the future. I would certainly insist that no assumption of that kind apply to me. I would certainly try not to be a virgin when I married; if that could not be helped, I would as certainly lie and declare that I was not one. Either way would prove my husband's love did not depend on my morals. That was the vital thing. I felt

~ 108 ~

original and determined. I only doubted, a little, my strength of character.

Meanwhile, one had to meet this odd discrimination. It was maddeningly upheld in classic novels. I have forgotten *Kenilworth* save for a picture in my mind of a room high in the castle, and a window, and a lady hovering either near or

Above: Terry in the wicker chair. ~ 109 ~

~ 110 ~ Terry and our
cousin Rob.

on its ledge intending to jump out of it, because a villain is advancing to rob her of her virtue. That at least is the scene I recall. And there indeed was the double standard which would have had her choose a death no hero would, attacked by a lustful lady. I would have had her die for virtue by all means, but not for this appalling imbecility.

And, later, when the changing times disowned the double standard, it nevertheless kept on interfering. In fact, another play we saw about the war, in its own way, out-Victorianed the Victorians.

We were older by that time, two wary girls, no longer in the charge of poor Miss North, and this time felt superior to an audience who seemed unaware of blatant nonsense.

Ann Harding, pale face held slightly lifted like a saint, and bright yellow hair satin-tight, played a prostitute who recently had given up her way of life because she loved a nice young officer and had promised to be true to him. This caused amazing trouble; both her officer and his men nearly lost their lives.

She was indeed in an awkward plight. Her beloved had been captured with his company, and there she was, in love with him, when the enemy commander took it in his head to spend the night with her. When she refused, the Prussian brute, in a spitting rage, threatened the instant death of every prisoner unless she changed her mind. Then came the vital point. Could she bring herself to do this? Those many lives hung balanced till she managed to decide, about two and a half acts later, to save them. It was a long and trying time for every member of the cast, and certainly for Terry and me.

Yet not at all for most of the vast audience, it seemed. Everyone around us was applauding, apparently delighted with the struggle of it all. Both men and women had accepted it.

★　★

A further curious confusion about sex, but limited exclusively to men, was revealed to Terry by a young, presumably enlightened man, who seemed thoroughly mixed up, poor thing.

Terry had jumped the gap to the age of beaux. I shared them, offstage, with impersonal interest. Local ones were uninspiring, but when they came from somewhere else, as Walter did, they talked intelligently. Walter and Terry used to quote Rupert Brooke back and forth and discussed philosophy, art, Freud, the theatre. One time he mentioned *Rain*, which Terry luckily had read. In fact, we both had, with sober respect. I remember Terry pointing out to me how the mountains of Nebraska, "curiously like a woman's breasts," were a symptom and a warning of the tragedy to come. She felt prepared to impress Walter and looked forward to it.

Then Walter, Yale man of the outside world—friend, *roommate* of the captain of the crew—said a lamentable thing. Teresa told me the next day, on our way to fetch the mail, down through the fields.

"You know the scene where Reverend Davidson falls in love with Sadie Thompson?" he had asked, apropos of some point of view, and had gone straight on about it while Terry, although too polite and shy to show her consternation, thought, "In *love!*" "Love?" Neurotic lust? Devouring frustration? Falling in *love* with *Sadie*?

Yet that was what he had said. Teresa carefully reported he had used that phrase that way.

"Oh, Terry! Do you really think he doesn't know the difference?" I exclaimed.

Teresa thought it likely.

The episode confirmed a tentative conclusion I had reached that men were not what they supposed. Whatever Walter meant, I had long ago concluded they got sex confused with love, quite unwittingly. It was easy to believe

~ 112 ~

that Walter's shattering remark was no mere slip of the tongue. I remember laughing with Teresa at the possibility; men were absurd that way! I have forgotten why I thought I knew so much about it. I only know I felt experienced, rather a *What Every Woman Knows* sort of sensation, or recognition, I believed, of alien innocence. Of course, this fortified my own immunity. I was glad I had no such taint, glad as ever to be wise. . . .

And then, on further thought, this fond assumption turned rather serious. Proper knowledge, considering the confused state of men, seemed to be a woman's responsibility.

Oliver with Beda.

CHATHAM

There is grass where the big house stood. For a while there were still the cellars, and the chimneys of course did not burn. Now the cellars are filled in, and the chimneys pulled down. I have a snapshot of nothing there.

It is not easy to assess the full disaster of the fire. There was the worst—the cruel—part which was all too real, overwhelming, absolute. And the lesser part, the total disappearance of the house, which also had to be accepted. And then the consequence of this, which, because I was away, I never completely took in till I was planning to go back, and started wondering where to stay—and if one would be welcome.

It used to be that wherever I was living in the world, I knew the house was there always. Even after Father died, when the house belonged to Bobbie; in fact, because of Bobbie, it was there to go back to.

The house seemed always to belong exactly where it stood, a quiet-looking place whose weathered shingles fitted in so naturally with its surroundings that from the distance it was hardly visible. It was on the south side of the road, which then dropped out of sight downhill beyond the farm buildings. The main entrance was reached by going round the north end of the Big Room wing, and then on to the porte cochere. The wide front door there opened straight into the hall, with the Big Room on one side, several small rooms and the staircase on the other. Father's study came first. Beyond this along the front was the kitchen wing. So the main part of the house was an oblong block. The dining-room wing projected west out of it from the bottom of the hall like the stem of a T. At its base was the glassed-in porch. Another porch, an open one on the south side, faced the garden—a sheltered quadrangle, protected not only by two arms of the house, but by a line of trees below and a wall at the bottom. The wall had a little picket fence at one end. And beyond this, safely hidden, was Mother's studio.

The house had had to be made smaller, though, after Father died. There was no more Big Room wing surrounded by its long verandahs; the porte cochere was gone; rooms were used in different ways. Yet the well-remembered objects, the familiar shapes and colors, made it look much the same. Some things had been transplanted. I found two favorite paintings, which had once been in the house in town, hanging in what was the dining—now the living—room, reassuringly at home there: the portrait of my mother looking at one quietly, that quizzical expression exactly captured, so that she herself seemed present, and a picture she had painted in her early married years of my father, a pleasing young man with sticking-out ears, reading to a bright-eyed little Bobbie, about three, sitting beside him holding an apple. The character of everything was wonderfully the same. And the house seemed indestructible.

I am forever glad that we were all there together one last time, through Bobbie's persuasion—glad of the man who took our pictures, all lined up in Mother's garden, Alice laughing till she cried, the man was so silly. Pitifully ignorant he seemed as well, poor thing, knowing nothing about any of us! I am glad to have a picture of those merry brothers and sisters posing nicely for an exasperated photographer who was painfully contending with the children we had been—behind the masks of grown-ups.

It was two months after that, late one night in December, when Bobbie and her husband were there alone, that the house burnt to the ground—with them inside it, and Murdoch, the dog.

No one knows how it began. There was an icy blizzard raging. The world was closed in fast against the storm. No one heard, no one saw, except two youths who were driving to New York down the frozen highway. They noticed the red sky to their right across the hills and made their way through the drifts and the howling dark, finally on foot, nearer the climbing flames, to alert the nearest neighbors. But by that time there was nothing that anyone could do but watch the fire take everything.

They say those poor scorched bodies may not have felt the flames—that smoke can smother quickly. Please God it did.

It took a long time after that to want to think again, and a long time to recall, without too much hurting, not only the lost dead as dead but as living in my mind, vividly alive there.

Now Bobbie is a welcome part. I can at last recall her with delight as well as pain, even with hilarity. I cannot help, thank God, but recollect her wicked grin. I remember her at table demonstrating the best way to spit out a cherry pip genteelly: having got it to the corner of the mouth, one listened brightly to the nearest conversation, tilting the head, nodding briskly in agreement, with a broadly open smile, until the pip fell out. I remember her beside me at Uncle Edward's funeral, shoulders shaking in silent mirth, having just pointed out to me in a low whisper something comic she had detected; or, in my very early school days, during a Christmas play, waving at me cheerily from the audience.

It is good to recall her now: her royal-blue eyes, her swagger, her elegance in old jeans, or impatiently dressed up, some long-abandoned hat pulled jauntily into fashion. It is in jeans I see her most. She was usually working, busy painting, with sensitive skill, a tray, a chair, a portrait promised that must get done—with expert care—and on

~ 116 ~

Opposite: Bobbie in the hollyhocks.

time. I can see her on the garden porch holding something on her knee that she is finishing. I can almost speak to her there.

She was often on that porch those latter years. It was as quiet there as it had always been. One still walked through the house to find it, and the bright garden beyond; the kitchen wing still made a wall behind tall trellises, though it had lost its upper story where the servants' rooms had been, and no mystic butler like Aeolian could look down into the garden on a dark night any more and behold two phantoms dancing.

Yet those many years later, on the porch beside that garden, Bobbie—slim, boyish, lithe—seemed hardly any different from when Terry and I were little, and she, supposedly grown up, came to climb trees with us. I was about ten perhaps, she about twenty-four, but that considerable gap never interfered. I never really thought of Bobbie as a separate grown-up person. She simply seemed an older part of Terry and me.

Selfishly I cherish her pure delight in this account and her stern demands that I continue writing it; and her insistence on a copy as far as it had got, which was to this final chapter. Her only wish in life just then, she claimed, was that she have it. "That," she wrote me firmly a few weeks before she died, "is all I want." It was on its way when the fire came.

Undertaking now to do what she admonished me to, still mindful of where we were last together on quiet days in summertime at that beloved house she died with, I think the most propitious way to start again is on that porch where I remember her most recently. It was a place where one was often read aloud to long ago. Terry and I spent hours there contentedly, on sultry afternoons, while Granny or Miss North was reading Dickens to us—to the impatience of a literary cousin who taught at Yale and stayed at Chatham most vacations. He bemoaned Dickens's style, which seemed idiotic of him. My only worry was the eccentric characters who were purposely one-sided. I used to wonder what they were behind their eccentricities. It seemed unjust simply to show a person's queerness, like dismissing someone drolly as "one of those people who," and leaving out the rest of him. I still remember gazing over Miss North at a tree, trying hard to reconstruct a character from *Our Mutual Friend*, to make him whole. Not to was a little frightening.

At the far end of that porch I had to stand still with a huge armful of flowers for long sessions, being painted by Professor Niemayer, a towering man we often discovered staying with us. He was head of the Yale Art School then, I think, a pleasant person, for us especially commendable because of a glass eye which we tried not to stare at but did, to see if it moved. His wife was often with him—little, in brown pleats. My brothers put them in the Bible joyfully. "And Professor Niemayer begat Mrs. Niemayer. And Mrs. Niemayer begat Professor Niemayer. And Professor Niemayer begat . . ." The glad tidings were unending.

I remember on that porch, at about the age of ten, being tried and found calamitously wanting. Dav and Ol had got a hold of a special test with questions suited to a child my age. The result was a disgrace. I was blatantly a halfwit. I remember both boys sitting on a hammock, while I sat facing them, repeating simply, "I don't know." "She doesn't know!" they cried, their voices breaking. I recollect their horror, and their glee—and me, laughing appreciatively with them.

I felt differently about other sorts of failure because of shortcomings which were all too real; and I longed to be delivered from two agonizing ones—my shyness and my mortifying stuttering. I recall being dismally reminded of them once. I was walking down a path between the grapevines feeling wonderfully happy; all was right with the world. . . . Then I remembered my afflictions. These had recently attacked me at a house where one encountered so much attention one felt rather on display, and made formal conversation. I was sent to play there sometimes, with the daughter, a friend by arrangement. That day's details are gone. I can only recollect a grand piano, dark; and a drawing room, light; and, bereft of feeling now, the bare fact of distress, with me stuttering and people listening. The whole scene came back to mind with wretched clarity, however, those few days later by myself among the grapevines, reminding me how I was made, confronting me with the sad fact that I had no right to feel so carefree— that what *seemed* like happiness would not be, *ever*—with defects like that.

My mind saves face, though, and forgets humiliation fairly well. I have forgotten other stuttering disasters except for telephone explosions like my asking please to speak to

"El-l-l-lizabeth," a close friend and cousin. What I recall are side frustrations, like the wish to read aloud to Teresa the way I could alone, and in unison at church, anonymous and free, with no one counting on me; or like my mother saying once that singing lessons ought to help, but that I must wait till I was older for them; or when someone else said, "Whistle first!" as if tight lips undid! Or like Teresa's reasonable counsel when we were striding through the laundry yard in town, off for a walk, with some nurse in a hurry. I must have spluttered something, for I remember Terry said, as

The house at Chatham.

we set out, "Count three before you speak." A child was cured that way, she told me, in a story she was reading. Or like things I knew were false: Teresa claiming that I hardly ever stuttered anyhow and my own relentless knowledge that she was wrong, of her madder proposition, too absurd to contemplate, that stuttering was attractive.

I have forgotten early shyness, too, excepting its discomfort; I know it was more physical to start with, a sort of animal exposure and an urgent need to hide, which foreran more conscious cowardice.

Despite these failings, what I thought could only *seem* like happiness could also be remarkably authentic. In fact, the world and I, as I remember them, were often positively blissful.

From the beginning to the end of being little, save for Christmas, that unequaled, marvelous interval, the best time was always summer. One was in the country, free— free to *play*, inspiring word! I remember running fast round the corner of the house at some early age, knees high, going full out, free in the summer air, the lovely day before me and countless more to come. This was probably in June, when one was blessedly aware of the spread of time ahead, of all summer waiting. The fall was ages distant with the day when there would be a dusty smell indoors all of a sudden, and my stomach would feel scared even before I recognized the smell as central heat, which meant school starting—when, while radiators clamored, uneasiness would grow into an awful recognition of time closing in. Enchantingly the opposite, a day in June was boundless and exhilarating. And free—with stockings shed! By then release had come. Permission to wear socks was intoxicating: "Mother-said-we-could-we-asked-her!" still rings gaily in my ears. We had put them on, and Miss North had discovered them. We had not risked her caution on that first warm day; we had waylaid Mother instead, unheard of and

~ 122 ~

daring! I remember Mother pausing in the hall, lips slightly pursed. "Why yes. I think so, dearies," she finally answered. And we bounded up the stairs to liberate our legs—and our hearts with them. Summer had really started.

Mother's voice then comes back clearly. I can see why Bobbie claimed the house was full of all our voices when she took it. I almost think she really heard them, and other people's too, and all sorts of bygone sounds. Voices from indoors and out; voices far and near; voices of grown-ups, voices of children, voices of dogs—all essentially a part of living in that place, back to the summer I was born there and must have listened from my crib beside the open windows to things like Sunday morning hymns with everyone singing, "Guide me, O thou great Jehovah; Pilgrim through this barren land," just behind the piano's lead. And I recall "There is a green hill far away," when I was older. I loved it, and told Mother so one day, a gratuitous disclosure that took considerable courage, but she said she loved it too. It was worth revealing.

Again I recollect the way her nice voice sounded—and Father's voice, as well, from upstairs somewhere, cheerfully calling, "Poly!", the name he fondly used for Ol, while claiming nicknames were abominable. And the way he used to whistle, blowing lightly through his breath, "We were sailing along, on Moonlight Bay" comes back as well. That lilting tune belongs entirely to him, and his footsteps with it, and a screen door closing.

In contrast, I remember Miss North humming far away, and Mother barely containing her impatience, exclaiming, "Children! If you feel like singing, *sing*. Don't *hum*. It's so exasperating!" Miss North's approach to many things was just as halfway. In church she used to sit while she was praying, leaning forward in the pew, instead of getting to

her knees. Mother found that equally trying.

Among remembered sounds are certain footsteps—one depressing time, Elleda's. I was having measles then and had been rushed out to the country on being noticed with dismay after Alice's wedding. We were on the point of moving out there, and I had to be moved fast to beat the quarantine, or stay in town. Rooms which had to do with me were opened up that night, and I was dispatched with Elleda in the limousine. She took care of me until they sent for a trained nurse. I cried hard when they told me she was coming, and I cried as hard again on the day she went away. Every change was heartbreaking.

But I remember Mother gladly, first to do with talcum powder—*Quelques Fleurs*, the lovely fragrance, the pretty bottle—she gave the nurse to use for me; then I remember, through the half sleep of a terribly high fever, someone gently rearranging me in bed and realizing with a surge of happiness that it was Mother. "I'm sorry to disturb you, little girl," she said, and I wished she knew how much it was the opposite.

But it was after I was sitting up in bed enough to play, and Elleda was once again in charge, that I recall the sound of footsteps. They were coming back upstairs, at last, after long listening. She had promised to return with some important object before she hurried off elsewhere; she was always on the run. Yet I had got my order in, and she was coming. I lay back content. I could hear her reach the passage. But then—unbelievably—she was climbing up the second flight of stairs, on up toward where her room was and, sick at heart, I knew I was being absentmindedly neglected.

Some sounds turn up together, like the noises I remember when I stopped a moment on the way downstairs: the sewing machine purring from the open sewing-room door; Terry's and my canaries frantically singing there; the lawn-

~ 124 ~

Opposite: my sister Bobbie.

mower's crescendo climbing up the slope outside; one of the maids talking. And if I picture myself reading out of doors on hot still days, the joggling, clinking rattle of a wagon driven slowly toward the barns comes back at the same time as the sound of distant thunder.

Thunder burst with deafening fury on that hilltop when it came. I tried not to be scared of the almighty crashes, and still remember when I was very young how I was discovered frightened during a storm. I was making my own way carefully along the walls of the Big Room, not venturing to leave them, my destination the front hall. I had reached the window next to the detective-story bookcase when Mother spied me and called me to her. She was sitting near the middle of the room. When I got to her, she picked me up and put me on her knee, with a little laugh as she spoke to someone. I had never been on Mother's lap before that I remembered. I was surprised, wretchedly self-conscious and uncertain what to do to keep her from regretting what she had done. I stayed absolutely still, legs tense in case my feet should slip down suddenly and hit her; and finally breathing because I had to, but as little as I could. The slightest move seemed wrong; she might notice my discomfort. This took considerable control, the kind that children often use, just as dogs do, with the same patience and wish to please. As a result, though in a different way than Mother meant, I forgot the awful thunder.

My mind turns back again to voices. Light, evening voices first. In the cool of the verandah and the dark—except the dim light from indoors and the fireflies sparkling—company sit softly talking. I am conscious of the murmur on the way to say goodnight there, and a small, attentive pause when I arrive till Mother greets me, and then Father, and I kiss them—then others, if expected to. One never knows, especially without their faces. In the darkness they are shadows that voices come from; I approach them by ear.

I recall a daytime clamor there, the screen door swinging wide as Teresa and I charge out, both boys behind us shouting, "It's a *Lily hunt!*" while we dash on ahead of them. We were off to find the Lilies, identical rag dolls. Mild but hardy, they survived repeated deaths. Our brothers branded them as dangerous at large and hanged them periodically, asking us brightly where we thought the Lilies were—which meant the worst; they were somewhere dangling.

And I remember another shouting charge from that same door—only inwards—when we were still "The Babies." At the count of three from Davidge, I burst out across the room to attack Terry coming from the screen door opposite. We met with full instructions for the assault from the two boys, each cheering his own man on. My orders were to aim at Terry's legs and try to pull them out from under her. And I had to come in shouting, "I'm too proud to fight!" like President Wilson, and keep on shouting it. Meanwhile Terry had instructions to grab both my arms or leap up my shoulders from behind, while trying to outshout me with another battle cry. We worked with splendid energy. And the boys called, "Come on, Babies!" and "It's a fight! It's a fight!" with rousing encouragement. They always chanted, "It's a fight!" when we were really quarreling too, if they happened to come upon us at it, and they sounded so delighted it was useless to go on; we could only laugh ignobly.

One sound comes back to mind peremptorily: the summons of the loud, staccato, cow-like blasts Ida, the waitress, used to blow through a long tin-colored horn from the edge of the east verandah. It called us from the barn when we were tunneling through the hay from floor to floor, or off the silo, or the icehouse elevator—or out of terribly tall trees no one but a child would climb, or off roofs breathtakingly perpendicular. It gave us enough warning to get back to earth again in time for lunch, looking tolerably respectable.

On the west stretch of the verandah, I can still recall Teresa's clear voice ringing with the stirring challenge, "We, the children of America, must shoulder the burden along with the rest!" It was the Win the War Club speech. Teresa had composed it, and those were its opening words. She made the same speech every meeting. We felt it could not be improved. It expressed our hopes, our sentiments—to us it was perfect.

Our club had three members: our summer playmate, Willie, the farm manager's small boy, Teresa, and me. It was a satisfying number; even Willie could hold office, though much the youngest and the most lowly.

Our single contribution toward winning the war was making candy from honey instead of sugar. We held meetings about it often, the sole item on the agenda except for one surprising time. Teresa, having delivered her valiant address, had just clambered down off the round white table where she always stood to make it, when to our amazement, Willie took the table too. He rose abruptly from the floor, where he and I always sat, and climbed right up and stood there. Then he told us he had written a poem about the war, and he read it to us with grave effort. It was a masterpiece; it rhymed; it made sense—we were overcome! He was clearly far more gifted than we thought; he had never shown creative skill of any kind before. "The Drummer Boy," he said his poem was. And so indeed it was. We came upon it later, word for word, title and all, in an old anthology. We were mortified for Willie, but relieved to be released from any thought of having to look up to him.

An operative voice from the gramophone indoors rang out at other times in that vicinity, singing "Goodbye For-

ever" to the people paying calls who used to sit on that verandah. The boys would turn the volume up as loudly as they dared, and then peer out of the window hopefully. Guests were frequently shown out there, as the coolest place to be. This was where Terry and I had often settled.

Above: still life of Chinese curios.

But they never found us there, only empty hammocks swinging crazily, all by themselves. We had always just managed to collect our things and sprint left round the rhododendrons.

Callers had to be discouraged, and were constantly avoided as menaces one might be called upon to speak to, or even worse for Dav and Ol, who usually had to show them the farm and all the animals. We ran away on principle, mistakenly sometimes: I remember Ol's chagrin on one occasion when he dashed down to the cellar away from what turned out to be his godfather with a birthday present.

Only Lady Grouitch, once, got a different reception. An ambassador's wife, she was accustomed to attention; nevertheless, what she got surprised her. It surprised us too, or rather Dav and Alice, stationed upon tables they had pulled onto the grass from the porch, to be better seen. I had gone with the contingent posted in a field on the opposite hill, and remember staring at our house far away among the trees and at some moving squares in front of it. Dav and Alice had flags, and they were signaling from there, and we were signaling back with flags too, a well-planned exercise. But then the car came up the road with Lady Grouitch in it, fetched from the station. Of course she spotted Dav and Alice at once above the bushes, on their elevated stands, flags waving, and to their dismay as the car approached the house, they saw her bowing and blowing kisses. Later, she told Mother how touching it had been to be greeted with such enthusiasm.

She was not the kind of visitor one minded, to be sure. When she came, she came to stay, and that was different. There were always people staying we met round corners and at table who rarely interfered and were often interesting. I can imagine the past voices Bobbie said she used to hear when she took the house, being theirs as well as ours. Lady Grouitch might be talking; she would be fun to listen

~ 130 ~

to, and Sir Slavco, her nice husband who enjoyed things and made jokes but could seldom get away from Washington. He was the Serbian ambassador, a tall, fine-looking man—a *good* man, Mother told us, having done such splendid things for his country and its allies that the king of England had knighted him. We approved of him particularly because he did not act as if he had to be a grown-up. He went swimming with us sometimes, and he would duck his head the way we did under the canoe, which we used to overturn to rise up into and look around, and hear how queer our voices sounded. It was a hollow, twilit place, smelling slightly of varnish and the cool lake water it floated on. I remember the dim presence of his head in that strange world, as interested as we were.

Lady Grouitch did not swim, or even walk really; I remember her explaining one ought to glide. She glided gracefully along exalted Serbian circles; she was a god-mother to Prince Peter as I remember it. American by birth, her life belonged to Central Europe. Its gaieties, its troubles, its particular gossip were interesting to listen to while she talked to Father and Mother. She made her world alive and her country beautiful. She talked well, and her eyes closed into half-moons when she laughed, which was attractive.

Alice heartily disliked her, as a chaperone mainly. But Alice must also have been maddening. They once sailed on the same ship, Lady Grouitch to go home, Alice to be a nurse in a Red Cross hospital—young, pretty, and independent. There were wild young men on board, off to war, though we were still a neutral country. These bold adventurers and the freedom of *jeunes filles*, in those days still unknown to Central Europe, must have made a trying trip for Lady Grouitch, poor soul, what with the added menace of real torpedoes.

Years later she returned and, at the time of the Second

World War, was a woman without a country—old, lost, and querulous, making rounds of endless visits to houses by then nearly servantless. She came for weeks to visit Father, with Elleda the sole staff to answer her needs and whims. Terry happened to be there, and ran her errands too, and helped her in and out of dresses, and patiently listened. But

The 4th of July village.

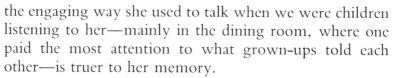

the engaging way she used to talk when we were children listening to her—mainly in the dining room, where one paid the most attention to what grown-ups told each other—is truer to her memory.

In sorry contrast was a peculiar visitor of mine who could not talk at all at table. She was no more than thirteen, but thirteen ought to have been reasonable. Not only was she speechless: when spoken to she giggled. I was miserably ashamed of her.

She had seemed all right at school—nice, amusing, usual, a friend to be, but outside of gym we had really only spoken while eating apples at recess. Yet I thought I knew her and liked her well enough to ask Mother if she could come and spend the night at Chatham.

I remember her two ways. First, inside a bathroom door, in shadow light, naked and unfamiliar. She seemed too white for one thing, probably because my limbs were tan; and her wet hair was greasy. I remember mainly the indifferent look she gave me as she stood there, bath towel in hand, and how flat I felt inside; and how I instantly detested her.

I had been trying to entertain her in an enormous shower-bath, an admirable diversion to Terry and me. The water came out sideways, from silver rings that rose in tiers around three walls, as well as downward. The acoustics were inspiring. There Teresa sang "God Save the King" in tune, though she was tone deaf. We stamped and shouted, I remember, in surprise and celebration. She had attained the unattainable. It was fun to splash and sing there while the water pricked and steamed and whished against the water-logged curtain, and fun to make it cold, so cold one had to scuttle out. But my guest showed no enthusiasm.

Next, I see her in the dining room, at table, beside Father, who was trying to converse with her politely. He would ask a pleasant question, and the rest of us would wait, expecting her to answer something; and she would pause and titter, her eyes sliding away. My heart sank while this was happening. I kept hoping she would pull herself together and make sense, the way one hopes a drunk will sober.

Who she was, or why so shy, and even rude and imbecile, I do not know; but she was sadly alien.

The most exciting noises of the whole summer came of course on the Fourth of July—loud, concatenated, satisfying, suitably in praise of that triumphant day; a day which always started in a haze of summer heat, and a flag at the foot of one's bed. And then, throughout the morning, the splendid banging came, and the great fun of making it—first, with little onion-shaped torpedoes, silver things that went off *slam* when flung down hard on the brick walk, then with firecrackers, riotously bursting right and left. On and on we hurled them. Then Dav and Ol stuffed packets of them into old tin cans and lit the fuses. Possessed by wild combustion, the cans would leap and hurtle in mad uproar on the drive, all hell let loose inside them.

That was morning. Everything was reasonably quiet after that until evening when the countryside had gathered and it was starting to get dark. Then, friends and neighbors, farmers, the Italians on the place and all the other men and all their families, and the guests who came to dinner, or had come to lunch and stayed, inspected the toy village in the north field; a proper village, on a street with trees and shops and houses, and people at their doorways and their windows. But every little house was stuffed with gasoline-soaked hay, and any moment something would ignite it. Then everything would burst into a raging blaze at once, flames roaring, hidden firecrackers banging. It began in drastic ways—a burning airplane, suspended on invisible black thread, dived down and hit a haystack that was standing by a barn; or a wound-up, tethered locomotive caught

fire and escaped, dashing madly to the station—swift disasters and reliable.

The village took weeks to make. We collected wooden boxes and then planks and all materials we needed from the storerooms in the barn, where we helped ourselves unhindered; and then paints from the laundry cellar, open cans with sticks inside to stir the colors into view. But that was at the finish. First we drilled and sawed and hammered in the carpenter's shop daily and industriously—the boys, Teresa, me, and our little comrade, Willie. Sometimes Willie's infant brother, George Arthur, was in tow and had to be tied up for interfering. Dav and Oliver would fix him on the end of a long rope, out of reach and howling. On the Fourth, when lunch was over, we lugged all the little buildings, wet with paint still, up the hill into the field, and laid the village out for burning. This ritual may well have been a bonfire to start with, when Bobbie was a little girl with Alice, before the boys were safe with saws and thought up better things to kindle, but for me it was a splendid matter of course.

After the village conflagration, the movies on the lawn, the ice-cream cones, and the gay procession with everybody waving sparklers till the great stock was exhausted, then carrying on with Roman candles (tricky things; we had to make sure no one held them wrong side up)—after the bustle of events and many voices, and when it was absolutely dark, a pinwheel swished, revolving slowly, and then faster. . . . Then another pinwheel started. . . . A single swoop, and the first rocket swept straight up to the sky, a shining ball up there as it bent over before detonating into multiplying sprays of colored light. Then rocket after rocket catapulted into stars and jeweled feathers and parabolas, in a crescendo of loud banging, till finally the last bright pattern burst and disappeared, gradually, in total silence.

The next morning went back steadily to being usual. The

~ 135 ~

noble Stars and Stripes were taken down, which Terry's grown-up hero, Sherborn Rockwell, had helped put up by climbing *easily* on the steep eaves. The centerpiece at table—little flags of every nation, which everybody tried to name at lunch—would be stored away again. The long table in the sinkroom, where the fireworks had been collected, would already have gone back to being where they fixed the flowers. We would search the lawns for discarded sparklers, which were disastrous for the lawnmower.

And it was generally raining on the day after the Fourth. They said rain came after gunpowder.

The great quiet following the last explosion of a rocket—that noiseless end to the noisy day—brings other moments back again in which the very lack of sound seems especially significant.

I remember long ago coming into the Big Room when nobody else was there, and making for the fireplace to take a furtive tug at a brick I had examined recently. It protruded from the rest and was definitely loose. I had once read a wonderful story about a little girl who had discovered such a brick, pulled it out, and beheld a lovely garden, into which she somehow got and found herself in fairyland. I knew it was a made-up story, and my faith in fairyland was pretty shaky anyhow, and I remember feeling shamefaced—yet compelled to see if maybe my loose brick *might* do the same. It was terribly exciting. Everything was still, and the stillness seemed portentous, as if it were expecting something magic; and my heart was beating fast. But the brick would only move the tiny fraction of an inch it had done the time I saw it first and touched it. I discovered there was nothing one could tug, no place to hold, quite obviously no way to dislodge it. So I went on my way. But that brief scene retains a curious sense of importance. I remember so exactly the capacious fireplace and the light

~ 136 ~

from the distant windows coming into the dark of the middle of the room—and that prophetic silence.

Once I silently watched a very old man. He was sitting in the garden on a bench, and I was in an apple tree, squatting on a branch, engrossed in my bird's-eye view of him. He

Above: portrait of Davidge's wife, Sonia.

sat absolutely still in the bright sun. His hair was white, the color of the bench. His face looked white too, above the black suit he had on. From where I was, the green grass framed him.

He was a clergyman, I think, staying with us a few days—a man who had appeared at table lately. The important thing about him from a child's view was that he was old and very fragile. In fact, Terry saw him standing with the firelight behind him and it glowed right through his ears, they were so thin.

Aware, then, from my tree that great age was before me, I was busy thinking over what it meant—the phenomenon of reaching the point where life and death are nearly meeting. It was fascinating. I was looking at a man too old to be one much longer, a person unavoidably ending. I tried to picture the procedure: almost nothing was still going on inside him, I imagined. His blood, colorless in white veins, was moving very slowly, would go slower all the time, until it stopped. This would be soon. I would never see the old man again, I decided. I did not mind, but it seemed curious. He died a few weeks later, and I overheard with some complacence what I already knew. Perhaps my accurate prognosis of the old man's end has kept the whole episode plain, but what revives it is the quiet of that long investigation, looking down between the branches, unobserved.

I made another silent analytic survey once—but in public—of a conscious victim sitting near me at the Belmont in New York, where Terry and I were lunching with Mother and Miss North; and where he was trying to. There is something almost unbearably still about a small child staring. Adults rightly feel uneasy exposed to an inspection as deliberately unhurried. Anything may be behind it. I was busy chalking up the sips of beer my man was taking, and carefully examining his face because I thought the hidden process that could finally make him drunk might change it just a little after every swallow. It might begin to look a bit elated any moment; I decided it was definitely redder. And undoubtedly it was. He could hardly fail to see me, and eventually acknowledged my interminable glare with a self-conscious smile-for-children. I turned away quickly.

Among other silent things I think of in connection with that house is a moment in the hall beside the staircase where I presumably concluded it was time to stop, having run that far by instinct. I had just been in a tree again, a poplar—bad for climbing, with useless branches facing the wrong way. One limb, however, slanted out enough to look worth trying, and I reached up to take hold of it. But I pulled my hand back fast. Something was moving up there, lightly; it felt rather like hair spreading. I had to stand on tiptoe to discover what it was: spiders, three or four big gray ones. They looked particularly evil, I suppose, in the dim light inside the leaves. Also they were unexpected; one must be prepared for spiders. They upset me, but it was not till later, when I had halted by the staircase after leaving them abruptly, that I knew I really loathed them. I could feel them again crawling underneath my hand. And I shuddered. Now shuddering was interesting, and I let it have its way, intending vaguely to try out the full sensation. It was a bad experiment. It swept me into panic; a sort of wild disintegration came so swiftly it was terrifying. I caught a glimpse of chaos round the corner of my mind. . . . Then I pulled out of danger. And I felt extremely cross about how stupid I had been. I remember thinking, "That's a lesson for you!" and deliberately, soberly, repeating to myself, "You must never do a thing like that again."

Other memories of silence are in places good for reading: fields, lawns, flat rectangles of roof, the top of the umbrella tree, all parts of the verandah on the hammocks, except during the war, when I was comfortably balanced on a chair

I used to tip against the wall there at a horrifying angle which made my lap a lectern, hands free for knitting socks for the Red Cross—thereby reading patriotically. There were quiet reading places in the rooms upstairs as well. I remember settling down in empty guestrooms, mostly for the novelty of unusual surroundings, with untried chairs for curling up in. But sometimes overwhelming things would happen in a book, and, above all if they were sad ones, the most dependable and reassuring spot was my bedroom. Inside that friendly place, with everyone downstairs too far away to hear a person crying, my heart could break quite privately. There, stricken by a death scene in *The Dove in the Eagle's Nest*, I remember such abandonment of sobbing as must, that day, have added to the waves of ghostly sound a child's lament for Bobbie's hearing. Sad stories about animals were hard enough to bear, like *Sans Famille*, but this was far worse, this was *brothers*. All I remember now are stone towers and green vines, and the two young men who were inseparable. And then one of them died and the other one was left *bereft forevermore*. I cried and cried. I believe I suffered then more than any other time throughout my childhood. While it lasted, it was agony.

But such moments vanished swiftly, surrounded as one was by real people in that friendly house. Like all rambling places children love and know by heart, it was variously played in and inhabited, from the coalbin where delighted captives waited breathlessly for the witch to pounce and haul in other prisoners, to the attic where the doll's house was that traveled every year from town to country with its occupants, and where the dress-up trunk was full of interesting things for trying on. I remember wobbling contentedly in satin high-heeled slippers that once belonged to Alice, dainty things—a child's feet nearly filled them. Up there in an adjoining room, Teresa found a box of Alice's

~ 140 ~

old letters—and at once we read them, admiring especially a note from a young man who kept "because, you see, I care" for the very ending.

There were interesting places and cheerful company, upstairs and down and often in-between at a variety of levels; stairs are comfortable to settle on and good for conversation. After coming home from parties—I was old enough to be included then with Dav and Ol and Terry—we often sat our way to bed, progressing slowly to the top in three- or four-stair stages. It was good to loiter there, and then to come to rest again and finish talking in the nearest bedroom—mine; I remember almost word for word what Dav was saying once. I was sitting on my bed, legs dangling, and he was standing by the mirror, speculating about things that made one listen carefully. He said he wished we knew what Jesus *did* as a young man, those several years before he started teaching; we knew he was a carpenter, he said, but nothing else. Did he marry? Did he fall in love? Did he have children? And then, a little later, I remember picturing the size of Earth, and maybe God, as he said lightly, "For all we know, the world may *really* be a corpuscle, in the blood of the veins of a giant."

Loitering to bed recalls the way the summer air would make a person want to linger, feeling the sultry night outdoors and seeing how wonderful it looked; for—in New England, where northern lights were often visible, and shooting stars and mysterious heat lightning, where, in the nearer blackness, fireflies danced silently, and the rest was secret—the effect was magical.

Once, long ago, on such a night, a little, private flame entranced me as it shone on human faces. During World War I an English soldier, Major somebody, I think, and a young woman, English too, were staying with us, and on that lovely evening I heard their quiet voices on the lawn where they were strolling in the darkness, fairly near where

I was standing, when the striking of a match revealed them to me as he lit a cigarette for her. Their heads were close together, hers bending to the flame that made their faces luminous, and very beautiful. The scene—gracious and intimate against the boundless night—still seems the essence of romance to me.

And it was gratifying too: I saw a pretty woman smoking exactly like the advertisements in *Punch* that made it seem a normal custom, which I liked to think it was, even in Connecticut. To be sure, I had found Mother with a cigarette one day in the library, and Father smiling at her, and after Dav was wounded in the trenches and came home discharged at last from a London hospital, he offered cigarettes to ladies. But I knew they would refuse, and felt ashamed of them and proud of Davidge. So I was thankful to be looking at a woman of the world who, naturally, behaved as she was meant to.

Unhappily, however, to behave as one was meant to toward the world included talking to it, and on one's own as one grew older, seldom knowing what to say. "I should try to think of *something*, dear. Anything would do, even 'What a lovely rose!' if they're on the table," suggested Mother apropos of some tongue-tied situation I had shamed her with—apparently at Chatham, for as she spoke I pictured the luncheon table there with roses on it, and myself delivering that unlikely declaration. Better far to suffer silence.

Yet the knowledge of incompetence would still be there, and a loss of dignity quite inadmissible. One had to bear it privately, the way Teresa did on one memorable evening. It was at the end of a long day after she had been meant to entertain an unknown boy as a gracious hostess. And it had gone so wrong that at bedtime when she was on her way upstairs and stopped to say goodnight to Mother, Mother mentioned it: "Dearie, I do think it would be nice if you

~ 142 ~

could talk a little to visiting young gentlemen." Teresa nodded dumbly. *Nice!* I suppose even our mother could not know, wise as she was, how nice poor Terry hoped it would be, nor guess the shame her mute child hid as she kissed her dutifully, nor the bleakness of despair, as she trudged to bed.

Mother had said the boy was coming, with his parents, family friends, and an elder sister; she explained it carefully. He was about Teresa's age; they would all arrive for lunch; then everyone would go to some baby's christening. There was a tacit, pretty flattering, recognition that Teresa was old enough to entertain a young male visitor. No need to ask her daughter to receive him suitably: it was understood. The thought was dizzying, and "Be on your toes!" implicit. She was not to be a child: rather, a damsel soon to greet her intended as she stood there listening with an air of appropriate indifference.

And so they came, and Terry found him seated next to her at table; and his sister opposite, unluckily, because he glanced at her it seems just before he turned to Terry and politely asked, "Do you go to Margaret's school?"

"No," Teresa answered.

"Oh," he said, "I thought you might."

Teresa pondered. Surely no such Margaret was among those senior girls one looked at coming out of classrooms and in corridors? She was pleased he thought her old enough for where his sister went, though. Some delightfully strange place, she reckoned, and was on her way to hazarding a vague sort of reply, when someone called his sister *Helen*. Terry's heart sank. A horrible foreboding about that school of Margaret's loomed before her. She started thinking, frantically. Could he then have meant *Saint* Margaret's, where in fact she *did* go? Had he maybe even *said* it? Could it turn out in the end his sister went there after all, she wondered wildly, and had seen her and told her brother, who only asked to have something to say? And was thinking her a liar? Or plain eccentric? It was sickening.

She might have plunged into the silence with some tangled explanation, or have laughed it off somehow; or have spoken with contemptible affectation of "a slight misunderstanding," but it was all too late—too late, in fact, to say anything. He thought so too; at least he never spoke to her again, nor did she speak to him, through the livelong day. Side by side they finished luncheon; side by side, on folding seats in the open car, they traveled to that christening, of no interest to either. Then, side by side again, they took their places for the drive back to the country, where finally it ended—that fiasco from the start—which for Terry seemed irreparable tragedy.

I recall myself too well in similar misery a few years later at a grown-up dinner-dance. It was in honor of a lively girl from the Channel Isles, who was all of twenty I suppose, like everyone except her younger cousin, a boy closer to my age, which seemed to justify my presence. Mother told me what to wear, which seldom happened. She said the dress was made of pretty stuff. Elleda had just finished it, a rose one made of voile and rather long, for room to grow in.

The day preceding this affair I went into retreat for a while, with a pencil and a paper, prepared to make a list of things to say when the time came. In the end it read "The Lake and Swimming." Nothing else we did all summer seemed to qualify; not that this mattered finally, because I hardly spoke that evening, if at all. I was sitting in the middle of a long row of faces, at a long thin table—with another row of faces opposite. I watched them gaily talking, and I suppose I ate my dinner. There was nothing else to do, no probability of speaking ever, what with a black forbidding shoulder plus a quarter of a back all I could see on either side of me, except a moment when I glimpsed out of the corner of my eye my right-hand neighbor turning

~ 144 ~

slightly toward me, and wondered if I ought to bring my chosen subject up, but was too late getting started.

The situation was much worse during the intervals of dancing. I think our numbers were uneven—a girl to spare—since everyone was on the dance floor then but me, the awkward youngest sitting with the empty chairs. I tried hard to look amused, as if the chairs were rather funny, and sipped water very slowly for something to do and to hide my face a little till my tablemates returned, and I could feel at least visibly included.

Finally, a year or so later, I got included orally in such testing moments—I had stumbled on a way to face disinterested boys and surprise them into listening. Talking nonsense was what worked. They seemed to spring to life, released. "Why, Uncle Barnabas, old top! How *are* you?" or any senseless sally brought immediate response: "Well! If it isn't Donald Duck!" No matter what, the mood was set, inconsequent, and I was free. I could hold forth light-heartedly in any direction. I remember ending up reciting Chaucer in the pantry with the Channel Isles girl's cousin one late evening. From way back at children's parties I had had a secret hope he might think I was worth noticing. So I was very happy sitting on the pantry table while he leaned companionably against the sink there. We had come to raid the icebox and were consequently eating, I suppose—but mainly talking steadily. I recall the fun of saying anything I felt like saying, of feeling entertaining and entertained, and the pleasure of a lovely, esoteric sort of sharing that came unexpectedly. "Whan that Aprille with his shoures sote ..." I had started, almost singing it for the lovely sounds, as with instant recognition he came chiming in, equally delighted.

But although nonsense got one talking in all sorts of pleasant ways, it scarcely took the place of valid conversation. I remember hoping I would talk about important things one day, and this would show that I was interesting. I pictured serious discussions by the fireside, where I would be expressing real opinions easily and sophisticatedly about some mutual concern. "Do you believe in platonic love?" for instance. Most important things to say though—and not just to scary boys, but to all respected people—were not expressible, and it would have been a pleasure to live up to family guests sometimes, by being reasonably articulate.

Not knowing how to put a thing, and so giving up, was what was mainly in the way, and most disheartening, especially when other people might have liked to hear the thing one would, if only possible, have told them, indeed dearly wished to tell them. I remember a sad case.

We were sitting in the glassed-in porch at Chatham at the time, Terry and I, with Mother and two visitors. Young Mrs. Rockwell, with a friend I felt most privileged to meet, had come to call. The friend was Rosamond Lehmann. And I had just read *Dusty Answer* with the utmost interest, but of course I never mentioned it, nor gave any indication of realizing who she was. Nothing seemed quite right to say to her, especially under observation. Unsolicited remarks from adolescent members of the family who happened to be present when company was there were never easy; one felt conspicuous. As this included Terry too then, and as Mother seldom paid much close attention to new novels or their authors, Miss Lehmann had no way of knowing she was recognized at all—and might perhaps have cared. It seemed a pity.

Hard as it was to talk to guests before an audience, it was worse without, and went on being so after I was quite grown up. My heart would always sink if I thought I might be going to be left with one. The most dangerous were strangers. They were always frightening. I recall an alarming instance, again at Chatham. I was waiting at one end of the Big Room, beside a door with people passing on their way to lunch—all but one young man, who stopped and waited with me. It was clearly up to me to say something. Moreover, it ought to be no ordinary comment, but something bright and witty, preferably a bit sardonic, which I thought he would appreciate. For I knew about him, knew of his meeting Terry at a lake in Canada, where she was visiting; knew the serious direction, the increasing certainty, that followed it; knew, indeed, I might be facing Terry's future fiancé, though to me the word itself seemed more appropriate to punctilious arrangements like announcements in the *Times*, and deplorably conventional. Tall, proud-looking, indifferent to everyone but Terry, politely reticent and rather frightening, he seemed apart from all of that. And in a category, too, unattainable to other aspirants: the young man with standard wishes about living in a house near enough New York for business, and "one maid to start with"; or the sentimental golfer; or the nice, poetic boy at Harvard, too short and too dependent; or even Walter, of the Yale elite, who had oddly said "in love" in reference to *Rain* and Sadie Thompson, but had such admirable humor; or the older, somewhat tiresomely eligible chap who kept referring to the status of his family as sufficiently "distinguished," and once hoped to marry Alice, and drove a sporty Marmon, and made Terry drive it; or the mercurial musician; or any of the rest. I could fault them all for something, but not this one.

I remember feeling agonizingly inadequate, and the panic of it, and the instant vacancy as everything stopped working in my mind; and laughing then in the silly way one does to fill a space up. And saying absolutely nothing.

That that stranger very soon became a friend and later, in welcome fact, a brother-in-law, may be why I still remember this so well. But almost any stranger scared me out of what to say. Almost nothing seemed appropriate.

Like most people scared of strangers, I was reasonably

~ 147 ~

brave, though, about accomplishing things in the outside world. I remember an unhesitating plan some years before about REAL LIFE, real life in capitals meaning something quite outside one's own secure environment, something foreign and invigorating. That time, it was a restaurant and I was a waitress in it. I pictured Childs near Fifty-sixth Street, I remember, and me in that excitingly plebeian, crowded place proceeding swiftly, an authentic part of it.

The vision came while I was sitting on my bed at Chatham once, with Teresa beyond the foot of it. We were bemoaning a predicament, a rut we had got into with local escorts; we were pretty desperate, because it looked as if the same two amiable, rather dull young men would be forever in attendance at dances and picnics and no one else would interfere. It was exasperating. Right then particularly so, what with Terry just having finished college, and me at large still after finishing the dutifully aimless winter of my coming-out party. There we were, in the last summer before becoming tied to any serious endeavors, an interval to make the most of in some satisfying way, unthinkable at home then. "New York," we said, a job there where REAL LIFE was going on, could fill the interim, and while we were discussing it, that waitress flashed in mind as if a curtain had gone up, revealing me, the indisputable protagonist, being called to crowded tables; taking orders; bringing them— giving everyone my deft attention.

Though that inspiration faded when other things to do at home kept interrupting, another plan got under way soon after that, on a higher plane but just as enterprising. Terry and I, the family willing, had decided we should go to Oxford, Oxford willing in regard to Terry, since it was she who held an excellent degree with which perhaps to qualify as a postgraduate student. I had nothing to commend me but a rudimentary course at the Sorbonne in Paris; I was an underling. I did, however, hope to tag along. I had a theory certain lectures might be open or sneaked into, specifically those given by Professor Quiller-Couch, whom I somehow transferred mentally from Cambridge. And if the lecture project failed me, I would at least be at large in that great city, and my academic sister would encounter men of letters, hobnob with distinguished minds over tea in private houses, and I could be with her. Above all, there would be students everywhere—*English* young men. In all, a worthy venture. I remember a long journey in the open touring car with Teresa and our parents to Dobbs Ferry for the experienced advice of the headmistress of the school, who knew the ropes. Sadly, that ended it.

This precipitated what had long been lurking in my mind. "You really should go on the stage!" I had been regularly told after performing in school plays, or just mimicking someone. It was a pleasant thing to hear, and flattering, of course. But that was all it meant, as I recall it, till at finishing school in Paris. At an opera matinée I was attending with a group of classmates, I was watching peasants dancing in a bright cathedral square, and my heart lifted, high and thrillingly. "*I* might be there!" I was thinking. "*I* may be up there some day myself! *It could happen to me!*"

It became a sort of challenge, weak at first, but finally so strong I even mentioned it to Mother. We were walking down the hill to church in town on a Sunday morning the following winter. I announced it awkwardly, feeling shamefully absurd, in fact outrageous, with no idea what she would think. She demurred only a moment, saying something about having always heard a stage career was difficult. And then she asked about my stuttering: would it bother me?

It indeed was still a nuisance but had never interfered once I knew a thing by heart, or at least its rhythm. It was during a first reading I might stumble. This I hid, then and

always, praying to be lucky with it. And, as things worked out, I was; although once I lost a part, at least a chance at it, just answering a question. I was in a casting office, and I was feeling fairly sure the interview had gone well. "Just give me your address," the woman said on my way out. Perhaps she spoke a bit abruptly. In any case, I felt a little hurried and there was a sticky word in it to be met steadily. I had had trouble telling it to taxi drivers fast enough, and other times as well; the word was "Grammercy." So when I got to it, it scared me. "Gr-Gr-Gr," I spluttered out. She sat there, staring, poker-faced. "Gr-Gr-Gr-Gr," I persisted, "Gr-Gr-Gr," till, at long last, "Gr-Gr-Gr-*Grammercy Park!*" shot out of me.

And, one dreadful day, I stuttered not just once, but on and on—during rehearsal in front of the whole company. I had been casually asked to read a part besides my own, in the absence of Miriam Hopkins. I was only to run through it, unobtrusively of course, for cues and timing. I began like a machine gun. Furthermore I kept it up. The scene was long, the speeches too; the result increasingly calamitous. And yet to stop would have acknowledged something odd was going on. I battled through, and the director let me—struck dumb, of course. Such antics coming out of a sane member of a cast of tried performers were, at the least, bewildering.

I never otherwise disgraced that proud profession by stuttering. When Mother asked about it, I predicted pretty rightly. But what mattered to me then was that her asking it at all meant she took my high ambition seriously. This strengthened my intention. It was then that I began to think about it realistically; and at the end of the next summer when those Oxford plans fell through, I made my mind up how to start, which school to go to. Come winter, I was in New York, not just because real life would be more interesting to see than provincial escorts, but for a long,

~ 150 ~

exacting training—determined to become, if I could, an authentic actor.

Teresa came as well. She had not decided yet exactly which to ply of all her many talents, so she took a course in typing to start out; I think because she fancied writing jobs the most, having once thought up one. She had figured theatre critics might need stand-ins to review the lesser plays. Her goal was Robert Benchley, who was still with *The New Yorker*, where she wrote him. He replied he had to do the work himself, regretting charmingly. Yet she hoped for something equally exciting. And it came—a different enterprise but just as interesting. That master of the scenic arts, Bel Geddes, gave a class in stage design that winter and Teresa joined it.

The end of growing up at home had virtually come then, since most of it went on in other places, and from that time on home, in town or country, was for going back to more than for setting out from. But it was good to find familiar things again when one returned; to feel well fed, well slept, thoughtfully looked after. I remember blessed times of coming back ill and being put to bed and taken care of, the relief of it. I took everything for granted coming home, from turning up in someone's car some eerie hour without notice, and with two or three companions, finding bed-rooms for them, and appearing—all of us—at noon for a hearty breakfast; to coming back the normal way some afternoon by train and being met and driven home in the Pierce Arrow; and finding things, at either house, the same; with Mother saying, "Nice to see you, dearie," in the hall most likely, and Father, "Hello, Chickie!" as I bent to kiss his cheek, having found him by the fire with his paper probably. And if later on, perhaps that evening, talking with them comfortably in the library in town or the Big Room at Chatham, they asked how things were going, I

could take for granted, too, that it was not to probe or interfere possessively. People had to bear in mind their children were not theirs to own, Mother once told me. She said, "Children are only borrowed."

And therefore we, released into the open world, were trusted there, and free, which was of course constantly encouraging; and although freedom was an obvious, inalienable right, one was proud of having parents who respected it, accepted one as independent. This I was, ostensibly.

But having grown up with Teresa and shared so much with her from the beginning, she was my counterpoint. Consequently, despite a stage career just starting which I had to face alone, and New York in the wild twenties— where I was managing myself with reasonable authority in unpredictable surroundings—it was she whom I relied on for the measure of most things, to weigh and appreciate them.

And I still relied on her for the measure of myself. Once I dreamed that she was dead, and it was horrible. I was in a gray place somewhere that was cold and limitless, and I felt disembodied there, forsaken, desperate. What most of me consisted of as far back as I knew, composed of both of us, aware together—discovering, comparing, doing, thinking about things, and remembering what no one else remembered—had gone. No other mind could recognize what mine contained. I pictured trying to explain and woke up crying.

I still depended on that sharing till, when I most needed to, I felt suddenly and reassuringly self-confident. It was at Chatham, on the glassed-in porch on Terry's wedding day, after the challenge of it ended. As maid of honor, I had felt pleasantly responsible for being on display and could put off thinking, for a good performance. Once departing voices and the slamming of car doors had stopped though,

and the aftermath had started, my mind began examining
what waited to be faced, and at last I could confront it
privately. The glassed-in porch looked quiet, so I went
there. It was where the wedding breakfast had been served

Above: our youngest aunt.

to the bridal party, and I had had misgivings about speeches, near the end. What if I, too, were supposed to say something? Now, later, that deserted place, with empty plates and glasses and abandoned napkins on the table still, looked just the way it ought to look for coming back alone to meet the mounting wretchedness stored up in me. ·

I stood, ready for the onslaught, wondering what it would do, rather curious about it. Then the fearful realization that Teresa was beginning her new role—had really started it officially—struck hard and deep. And wounded. And the dread of finding out that I was left with only me was the deadly part of it.

Then, I was looking ahead calmly, I discovered, picturing tomorrow back at work, how it would go. And all at once I felt alert. Something kindled, and a feeling of attainment lit up wonderfully in me with a sense of what was coming. It was like the time when I was little, climbing up the cellar stairs and "someday you'll be twelve" shone in my head. That sense of purposeful awareness, and of me moving on, was there again, the future luminous. And the room was shining too—the utter brilliance of the light coming through the trellised glass of the walls comes back to me as if it were related to myself. "I'm all right!" I thought, and the world was too.

And that vivid knowledge seemed to be a present God was giving, I remember, and I thanked Him gratefully— "whether He is real or not," a baffling concept, yet it always worked for feeling honest either way with Him.

And then, perhaps because real gratitude on any terms releases, I was thinking about Terry and her husband, of their starting off together, man and wife from that day forth—that great, unforeseeable adventure. "O dear God, please make them happy," I whispered, "always." Each word may not be accurate but seems to come exactly as I meant it, and by then there were no strings attached

addressing Him. I spoke directly from the bottom of my heart, then waited, still, till it was as if He heard me. I think He did.

Of course, I made an ignominious descent to me again, all too immediately impressed by the touching picture I made standing there and praying, all alone, and all dressed up. Stupidly, there was a stinging in my eyes. I remember its intrusion as I turned to leave the room on my way to pack and change. And I remember proceeding slowly through the dining room, the hall, and up the stairs, and my relief that nothing dire had become of me.

And that I was adequate. This above all, for not to be is the most fearful of all worries, related to essential matters like survival, and competence, and faith as a conscious person. The enormity of being single in creation is pretty frightening, of course, and an awful threat to self-sufficiency. For me it meant extravagant concern with nothingness. As I see it now, that nihilistic dread which terrified me in the nursery with the possibility that there was nothing anywhere beyond my consciousness came back turned outside in—to fear of nothingness in me. It was still a bleak negation, a tenacious one.

It was the feeling that my self, all on its own, was incomplete, that it depended for validity, indeed existence, upon outer recognition, mostly Terry's, but in essence any recognition, the way vibrations can only be converted into sound by a receiver. I had heard it stated that a tree, if it falls deep in a forest and, convenient to the premise, there is nothing there to hear it, will fall *soundlessly*. I suppose the barren outcome represented what I dreaded, was like what I might be made of—might be me.

On the day of Terry's wedding, knowing I would be exposed to feeling more alone than I had ever been, and afraid to think, that same discouraging sensation of confronting myself separately, and finding nothing there—or not enough to be a person—was what I expected to be threatened with. And when that sudden light recurred and brought the certainty of self-significance on earth and exciting membership, it was so wonderfully opposite and heartening, I felt not only whole—much more than that— acceptable.

And that was when the independence I professed became, I think, as true in spirit as in practice, and deserved its name.

"Society girl opens in a new play," *Variety* announced soon after this. Though it embarrassed me to be presented in that fashion, I remember feeling pleased in a rather guilty way that it was newsworthy, but unashamedly delighted of course with the prestige of special mention in that oracle of Show Business. And discovering my picture in the *Sunday Times* that week, the same size as Walter Hampden's, adjacent to it and looking equally important, delighted me as well. I was proud to be in such exalted company.

Here, these memories of Chatham long ago may best be left, with Teresa married, and Broadway ahead of me. They have wandered far afield but always back to the same place where things still come to mind so vividly.

Perhaps what happens in the summer is what stays the most distinct—even small events are heightened then, it seems. I suppose a sense of freedom that no other season gives is partly why; and gentle weather, an emotive thing— an exciting feeling of immediacy comes with balmy air. Also—and blissfully—for all the years one is a schoolchild, summer represents a stretch notably measureless of time for playing in. But I believe where summer was when one was young recovers most of what it meant then; and, of course, for me this mainly has to do with Chatham.

Now, envisaging it all, renews a moment with my father

there. It was on the long north drive—we were out riding, he and I, and he stopped his horse and gazed across the land he loved, and said how well it looked but it was hard to keep it so, that times were difficult; he said the farm was losing money, he would be poorer when he died and would have less to leave us, but he felt that the pleasure this dear place was giving us while we were young was more important. And then he added reflectively, "You'll always have this to remember."

While I was listening, sitting still there on my pony, staring straight ahead of me at the far hills, I thought how one day I would be way out beyond them facing unimaginable things like Father's death that he had spoken of so easily; and the world, and living in it, were too full of grief to bear; or so I felt, till those few words about remembering brought me back to what I knew, and where those memories would be—aware of both dear places where I lived, the life they held. I had a sort of bird's-eye view of all my youth in them. And it made me feel contented, so rewardingly that it must have been what Father had in mind a little too when he was thinking of the pleasures of recalling things.

Out for a drive.